OVERCOMING SOCIAL ANXIETY AND SHYNESS

BUILD YOUR SOCIAL CONFIDENCE, INCREASE HAPPINESS, MASTER YOUR FEARS AND MANAGE PANICK ATTACKS

Perry Williams

CONTENTS

ABOUT THE BOOK--1

INTRODUCTION--- 2

CHAPTER ONE ------------------------------------ 5

Anxiety --- 5

CHAPTER TWO ------------------------------------ 11

Generalized anxiety------------------------------------11

CHAPTER THREE ------------------------------- 29

Social Anxiety Symptoms------------------------------29

CHAPTER FOUR------------------------------------ 38

Defeat Social Phobia Without A Psychologist---------38

CHAPTER FIVE ----------------------------------- 54

Overcoming Social Anxiety ----------------------------54

CHAPTER SIX ------------------------------------- 66

How to Overcome Shyness -----------------------------66

CHAPTER SEVEN ------------------------------- 81

How To Stop Panic Attacks -------------------------------- 81

CHAPTER EIGHT---**91**

How To To Increase Your Self-Confidence----------- 91

CHAPTER NINE ---**101**

Emotion Anxiety --101

CHAPTER TEN ---**113**

How to Control Emotions ------------------------------113

CONCLUSION -- **125**

ABOUT THE BOOK

OVERCOMING SOCIAL ANXIETY AND SHYNESS: Build Your Social Confidence, Increase Happiness, Master Your Fears And Manage Panic Attack

When you suffer from anxiety, you are not alone, you know that symptoms can occur anywhere, anywhere. Relief is here. Be cool to eliminate symptoms when they strike with state-of-the-art strategies that allow you to reduce anxiety on the spot.

The book is both a helpful way to manage stress and a close look at depression triggers. Evidence-based approaches show you how many different circumstances will affect a variety of symptoms. You are always prepared with Be Calm

INTRODUCTION

When you have social anxiety, you avoid social events for fear of being exposed to scrutiny and the observation of other people. The demands of acting correctly and not making a role in front of other people are of such magnitude that you prefer to avoid social events. There are treatments to combat social anxiety.

Before social anxiety was known as social phobia and resembles a phobia in which the fear of something is so strong, that it becomes impossible to approach this something. As with other phobias, it can be practiced to eliminate avoidance and fear, but gradually and in a safe environment. Social anguish refers to the anxiety that arises from being exposed to social situations where you risk being overwhelmed by feelings of shame and dislike.

How does it feel to have social anxiety?

Maybe ideas like "I'll be a laughing stock", "everyone will look at me" or "everyone will think I'm crazy" come to mind.

At the moment, anxiety can be expressed physically with tremors, palpitations, dry mouth or blushing. You may feel that you are going to pass out or lose control.

Body reactions are the result of the reaction of your nervous system to a situation that is interpreted as a threat.

You can have the urge to get out of the situation as quickly as possible.

How does it affect your life?

Social situations end up being too unpleasant when you expose yourself to them. Just thinking about being in the center of the attention of others feels unbearable.

Avoiding social situations can lead you to be increasingly isolated. Avoiding complicated situations can be a short-term relief, but the long-term anxiety worsens. The more space you give to anxiety, the less space is left to live the life you might want to live.

When should I seek help?

If anxiety about social situations restricts you in your daily life, you should ask for help. This is also true if you self-medicate with alcohol or tranquilizers to cope with everyday situations.

What kind of help can be received?

There are treatments to combat social anxiety. You could talk to someone who can help you understand more about yourself and why you react in different situations. You could also receive group therapy. It may be necessary to be under pharmacological treatment for a period.

We are all different and the treatment that works for one person may not do it for another. It may be necessary to try until you find what works for you. If you have previously sought assistance, but consider that it did not work, you should not give up, you should seek help again. Research has shown that what determines the success of the treatment is not the type of therapy, but the relationship of trust established with the trafficker.

CHAPTER ONE
ANXIETY

Anxiety is a natural reaction of the body to threatening situations and constitutes a kind of survival function. Different degrees of anxiety can be experienced, from diffuse worry to strong body symptoms or a feeling of panic, as if one were to pass out. Anxiety is always temporary, but it can return.

How does anxiety feel?

Anxiety can be felt in different ways depending on the person and can vary in intensity. Faint anxiety can be felt as worry, restlessness or a sense of unreality, of being in a "bubble." Strong anxiety can be felt more in the body. Breathing difficulties, chest pressure or palpitations may occur. If anxiety appears quickly and suddenly it is called panic anguish, and what happens when anxiety arises is a panic attack.

When anxiety arises, it is common to think "this will never happen" or "I'm going crazy." When you feel that, remember that it is not true! Anxiety is always temporary and not dangerous, even if you feel that way at the moment.

Why do I experience anxiety?

Anxiety can be triggered, for example, by a thought or sensation that scares you, or that makes you feel threatened, helpless, unsuccessful or worthless. Sometimes anxiety is linked to high demands or feelings of shame or guilt. It is common to feel strange or weird, that there is something "wrong" in one.

Anxiety can also be triggered by suffering disappointment or abandonment. The risk of losing something that is important to one, for example, security, status or love, can also cause anxiety.

What happens in the brain when I experience anxiety?

Anxiety is an uncontrollable reaction of the central nervous system. The reaction is a kind of alarm system that is activated when the brain and nervous system react to a threat or danger. The danger is not always real. When the brain sends signals that life is threatened, the body reacts and experiences itself as anxiety.

The sensitivity of the alarm system will depend on the person and may vary during the course of life. It is not unusual to feel more anxiety in adolescence and early adulthood, and less when advancing in age. Anxiety sensitivity can also be affected when living in complicated situations.

What type of treatment can I receive?

All treatments against anxiety involve learning to manage anxiety. Therapy is called exposure and implies that you, being in a safe situation, gradually learn to endure the feeling of anxiety. When you manage to control at the moment, you will notice that it disappears by itself after a short time. Through exposure, the sensitivity of the brain's alarm system can be adapted and thus be less exposed to anxiety.

Is anxiety common?

We all experience anxiety sometimes in life, some more than others. Although anxiety is very common, few people talk about it openly. Therefore, many associate anxieties with feelings such as shame and guilt. Since anxiety is not seen on the outside, people believe that only they live it, making it difficult to talk about it more than it should.

Many hide that they have anxiety or act as if it did not exist. The more you try to avoid it, the harder it will be to handle it.

How can anxiety be managed and what can I do?

It is natural to want to run away when anxiety arises. It is human to try to avoid discomfort. But anxiety does not disappear when trying to avoid it, on the contrary. A good way to handle anxiety is to accept it, enjoy the situation and not try to run away from it. If you can bear it, anxiety usually disappears faster and will be easier to handle in the future.

It helps to talk to someone about how you feel. Often talking is the first step to improvement. You can also learn more about anxiety by reading about it and how to treat it.

Many times, stress and anxiety are paired. If you try to eat, sleep and do activities that you like, you will generate greater resistance to both stress and anxiety. Another important thing is to dare to say no and limit what you are able to do.

What is an anxiety disorder?

When anxiety affects your daily life, it can be an anxiety disorder that should be treated. For example, a panic disorder, generalized anxiety disorder, social anxiety disorder or phobic disorder.

When should I seek help?

If every day you feel so anxious that this affects your life, you should seek help. Do not see it as a failure; courage is often required to ask for help, and the sooner you do better. If you don't want to ask for assistance anyway, ask someone you trust to help you with it. If you don't have someone you can trust, you can call or chat with someone on the support line anonymously. Here you will find a list of organizations that you can contact.

What are mental disorders?

Psychological discomforts, for example, worry or depression, could constitute normal reactions to life-threatening situations and are often temporary. It is important not to pathologize what constitutes normal reactions to life events; At the same time, early identification of psychiatric conditions could have a positive effect on prognosis.

Mental health according to WHO

There is a debate among scientists about the concept of mental health. A common denominator is that there are several dimensions of well-being, for example, emotional, psychological and social. According to the WHO definition, mental health is a condition of psychological well-being in which an individual can perform, manage normal stress, work productively and contribute to the society in which he lives. Therefore, mental health is more than the absence of mental disorders and includes both the experiences of the individual and the relationships between the individual and their social environment.

Mental health and mental disorders can coexist

The definitions of mental health are vague, but most agree that it goes beyond the absence of mental disorders. Mental health is described as a condition where several dimensions of the individual work well, thus feeling the individual joy and well-being with himself, with others and in his relationship with society. According to certain scientists, mental health and mental disorders can coexist in an individual.

How is a mental disorder diagnosed?

Severe mental disorders are psychiatric conditions that are expressed in a syndrome, verifiable from different diagnostic criteria. An example of a diagnostic system is the WHO International Statistical Classification of Diseases and Health-Related Problems (ICD). Another extended diagnostic system is the Diagnostic and Statistical Manual of Mental Disorders (DSM), published by the American Psychological Association (APA). DSM manuals are used in clinical practice also outside the US; However, the official system for establishing diagnoses in Swedish health services is the CIE.

CHAPTER TWO

GENERALIZED ANXIETY

If you feel so anxious that all the time you are thinking that something horrible is going to happen, you may have a generalized anxiety disorder. It is also known by the acronym TAG.

What is it like to live with generalized anxiety?

Living with generalized anxiety is like having the catastrophe radar constantly. You may feel that you can never rest from worry and almost never manage to feel really safe. As soon as a disturbing thought arises, you feel the need to clarify it immediately. You may feel that you should avoid all emotional discomfort and have difficulty living in the moment.

It is common to present other psychic or physical ailments simultaneously. It can be obsessions, eating disorders or depression, or constant pain in the abdomen, back or shoulders. You may feel dizzy and disoriented and have ease of crying.

GAD is one of many anxiety disorders and it is common to present several of these simultaneously. Among the other anxiety disorders are social anxiety, panic disorder, and phobias.

How does it affect your life?

You may have sleep disorders and sensitivity to stress, separation, and situations where you could lose control.

You are often worried about everything from near catastrophes to the situation in the world. Almost everything can be perceived as a threat and you may feel a huge need for security. Constant stress and anxiety could lead to the funnel of exhaustion or depression. The more space anxiety is taken, the less space is left to live the life you might want to live.

When should I seek help?

If the anxiety is such that it prevents and restricts your daily life, you should ask for help. This is also true if you self-medicate with alcohol or tranquilizers to cope with everyday situations.

Do not hesitate to ask for help if this is your reality. There are many things you can do to feel better, and the first is to seek medical assistance. If you don't know where to ask for assistance, you can look for an office.

What kind of help can be received?

A treatment could make you feel better. There are many types of treatment, for example, talk therapy and medical treatment. The treatments are intended to teach you how to handle anxiety so that it does not affect and does not restrict your life.

If you have previously sought assistance, but consider that it did not work, you should not give up, you should seek help again. Research has shown that what determines the success of the treatment is not the type of therapy, but the relationship of trust established with the trafficker.

Many people have lived with anxiety for many years, but have found a way to feel better.

Life is not over knowing that you have a diagnosis or perhaps several, on the contrary. It could give you a greater understanding of yourself and make you take yourself seriously, and help you understand what you need. It could make you stronger and improve your self-esteem.

When you gain an understanding of your difficulties, it could give you a chance to feel better. The above could teach you other ways of relating that allows you to set limits to your concerns, and let trust in relationships or broader contexts emerge. The more you manage to let go of control, the better you will begin to feel.

Types of social phobia:

- Simple social phobia: it is a phobia that is produced by a traumatic social event, and that is maintained over time, but with an easy therapeutic approach and a very good recovery.

- Social phobia with obsessive traits: It is the most frequent, it is a type of phobia that is not acquired by a traumatic situation, but develops due to obsessive personality traits along with some traits of shyness. Its treatment is more complicated than a simple phobia, since it is necessary to make a mixed therapeutic and pharmacological treatment but, normally, they have a good prognosis.

The most effective treatment for social phobia, based on our clinical experience, is a combination of cognitive therapy along with medication.

Since social phobia is a phobic-obsessive problem, both recurrent thoughts and the emotional response associated with certain interpretations of social situations must be treated. This therapeutic approach allows a complete overcoming of the social phobia

DEPRESSION

Feeling sad or unusually tired is sometimes not strange, it is part of life. But if nothing moves you or causes you pleasure for a prolonged period, you might have depression. There are treatments to fight depression.

What is depression?

If you feel sad, decayed and exhausted every day for at least two weeks, it could be depression. Depression is a disorder that changes the way you think and feel.If you have depression, it is common for you to get irritated easily and have concentration problems. You may also have difficulty making decisions, anxiety and sleep disorders. You may experience life as difficult and meaningless.

It is common to think that you will never feel good again, you could even become convinced of it. Thoughts may arise that you are a failure and useless, and worry about how your environment would react if you told how you feel. You may feel that you keep a mask and that behind it you feel that everything has fallen apart.

Even though you feel so bad, you often don't understand that you are depressed. Instead, they are convinced that the ideas of the nonsense of everything and suffering are the "truth" of life. Although for the moment it seems to be like that, depression makes you forget what you really enjoy in life. In this way, depression "lies" to you.

Different degrees of depression

Depression can be mild, moderate or severe. If you have mild depression, you can often endure every day despite how bad you feel. In moderate depression, everyday life becomes more difficult to cope with, but you can do the most necessary. In severe depression, you just get out of bed. In this situation, simple things like making a call or opening the mail become impossible.

Then, thoughts may arise that you can't stand living anymore. You cannot see an end to your suffering and you are convinced that you are the only one who has these feelings. The idea may also arise that it would be better for your closest ones that you were not. If you feel this bad, you should not be alone and you should seek help immediately.

Help is at your fingertips

If you think you have depression you should seek help in medical assistance. You will find an office in. If you do not want to be the one asking for medical assistance, ask someone in your area to contact the assistance. If you feel so bad that you have thought about committing suicide, you should not wait and you should seek immediate assistance, in a psychiatric emergency .

What I can do to feel better?

It can be difficult to have the strength to take care of yourself when you have depression. No matter how difficult it is, it is important to eat and sleep. Try to go out every day, if only to buy a block away. It is better to quit alcohol, even though it may relieve at the moment.

Talking to someone, writing or listening to music can be ways of feeling better or at least less bad. Depression is often temporary but may return.

It is important not to interrupt a depression treatment early, even if you feel much better.

You're not alone

Many have had depression and have known how to get out of it. Today, depression is one of the most common reasons for sick leave. Being on sick leave is not a sign of weakness or failure, quite the opposite. It is a way of giving you a new opportunity to be well.

FUNNEL OF EXHAUSTION

Today, stress-related illnesses are the most common reasons for sick leave. When stress is too much, the risk of developing funnel from exhaustion arises. It is a disease from which it takes time to recover in body and soul, and whose warning signs must be taken seriously.

What is the exhaustion funnel?

The exhaustion funnel is the result of prolonged chronic stress, which has lasted a minimum of six months without sufficient recovery. Previously it was called professional attrition syndrome, and it implies an overload of the brain and sickly stress.

The exhaustion funnel is divided into three phases. The first is the prodromal phase, which generates physical and psychological symptoms of overload, but the person can still function daily. Here, most understand that the symptoms are due to excess stress and change their lifestyle.

If nothing is done to remedy the situation, you risk entering the acute phase. This phase often occurs quickly and explosively, hence the expression «bump into the wall». The acute phase can last a few weeks, where nothing works. It may be impossible to get out of bed, think clearly or concentrate. The ability to do several things simultaneously disappears. Emotions of despair and panic may arise, which could be misunderstood as depression.

The third phase is the recovery phase. Here the affected person stops again, but he is still very tired, sensitive to stress and has difficulties in concentration and memory. The longer the recovery lasts, the better the person will function again in their daily lives. The exhaustion funnel always implies an increased sensitivity to stress, even when other symptoms have disappeared.

How does it affect daily life?

80 percent of those affected are women and, often, they are not the people that the environment expected to get sick. The person is often committed and skilled in

their work, assumes responsibility for their family and always puts the needs of others before their own.

The symptoms of stress are varied. They can be expressed in physical symptoms such as back pain, headache, stomach, and intestinal discomfort, palpitations and low immune defenses. The person may be tired, but at the same time, has difficulty relaxing and sleeping. He feels worried, anxiety, and depression, and has difficulty concentrating.

Why should I seek help?

It is important to listen to the body's warning signs and seek help in time. Returning after exhaustion can be difficult and take time, but the sooner medical help is sought, the less damage the disease will cause. No one will thank the affected person for having endured so much before getting sick.

If you or a family member is in the risk zone of a stress-related illness, you should seek help in an outpatient or in the company's health care. In the case of acute symptoms, we recommend a psychiatric office. A doctor will perform a body exam and listen to your story about discomfort. Blood tests are often taken to rule out other diseases.

Most people who suffer from exhaustion funnel recover, even though it may delay and involve increased sensitivity to stress. There is also a risk of relapse. The affected person must be on sick leave or reduce the workload to give the body a chance to recover. It helps to perform relaxation exercises, exercise and sleep well. The requirements must be reduced, time to share with friends and family, and do things to one's liking.

The treatment may consist of conversational therapy, preferably group, or drug treatment. The important thing is to remember that drugs are not the solution, but an aid to face the real reason for stress.

PSYCHOSIS

In a psychosis, you find yourself in a situation where you cannot distinguish between your ideas, your fantasies and the objective reality around you. You could suffer from a transient psychosis, called reactive psychosis, or develop repetitive psychoses as part of psychiatric diagnosis, for example, schizophrenia. Most people who suffer from psychosis recover over time, completely or partially. Receiving treatment decreases the risk of new psychosis.

What does a psychosis imply?

Experiences during a psychosis are not real for other people, but they are for you. The "imagined reality" is called, in other words, delusions or hallucinations and can mean, for example, that you hear voices or experience other phenomena that others do not see. In a psychosis, thoughts are transformed into an absolute reality that is not open to discussion. Different people may react differently during a psychotic episode, depending on the situation, personality, and circumstances.

Changes in self-image and perception of reality during psychosis

The object of delirium may be the person himself. It is common for the psychotic to perceive himself as changed. A psychotic person could, for example, believe that he is a historical person, representing evil or other qualities. A psychotic person could be enraged and want to confront their surroundings, another feel like a savior and want to hug everyone around them and the third turn to themselves and isolate themselves. The environment seems absurd or unpleasant

Conflicts with the environment in a psychosis

The perception that the environment does not understand what you are talking about and does not share your concern or does not see things that seem obvious to you can be very frustrating in the eyes of a person with psychosis. That is why psychosis often implies a conflict with the environment.

Why is psychosis?

It is not established why some people have psychosis, but there may be an individual predisposition due to genetics, parenting or particular traumatic events. There is also a relationship between drugs such as hashish or marijuana and psychosis. The predisposition to psychosis increases as there is a great lack of sleep, anxiety, hypomania or depression. If you have repeated long-term psychosis, you have a disease that must be treated.

What kind of help can I get from a psychosis?

Before receiving the indicated treatment, you need to undergo a psychiatric evaluation. Depending on the problems you have, different treatments may be necessary, such as pharmacological, therapy or other psychosocial support. To get good assistance, it is good to have a medical assistance plan.

Most recover after psychosis

You might need support and help from your environment to recover. You need to understand what has happened to you and what you should do to avoid returning to the same. You may need to medicate for a prolonged period, as well as recognize the early signs of psychosis and know how to get in touch with medical care to avoid a new psychosis.

Emotional instability personality disorder, SIT

Emotional personality instability disorder (SIT), or borderline, as it is also called, describes the problems you have if you are emotionally unstable, full of anxiety and show a pattern of self-destructive behavior. If you have TIE you could reach a state at the limit of the psychotic, where you doubt everything, both of yourself and others. Alternate quickly between different emotions and you can move from despair to euphoric joy in a very short time.

It is common for you to feel very bad and feel very embarrassed to have these problems. But you are not alone and there are specific treatments for SIT. There are also many things you can do on your own to feel better.

When you have an SIT, it is difficult for you to handle emotions of abandonment, anxiety or anger, and it is common for you to harm yourself in different ways, either physically or psychologically. Sometimes you can feel acceptable self-esteem and, at the moment, descend into deep self-loathing. Many people with SIT describe a feeling of emptiness and identity problems.

If you have a TIE, you may have difficulty feeling confident and secure in close relationships, and often oscillate between the admiration and repudiation of people closest to you. This can make it difficult for relationships to extend over time.

It is common for you to "self-medicate" with alcohol or drugs, or to develop eating disorders or harm yourself.

How to know if I have a TIE?

According to the established criteria, they must meet at least five of the following symptoms:

- A deep fear of being abandoned.
- A recurring feeling of emptiness.
- A confusing or unstable self-image.

Strong oscillations between different emotional states: Strong irritability, anxiety or depression that lasts for hours, even days.

Stormy relationships that oscillate between deep admiration and extreme contempt.

Intense and energetic anger that says nothing about what triggers it.

Brief, exaggeratedly malicious ideas, or transient emotional experiences of being out of reality.

Impulsivity that results in, for example, drug, sex, food or money abuse.

Self-harm, suicidal thoughts, speech or plans to take your own life.

Even if you feel identified with these symptoms, it is not certain that you have an SIT. To know if you suffer from a TIE, it is necessary to undergo a professional evaluation. It is important to rule out that symptoms are due to other reasons.

Many people with borderline disorder have experienced very traumatic or chaotic upbringing. Some have suffered abuse. But you could also develop a TIE despite

What kind of help can be received?

Having lived a healthy upbringing, with no apparent trauma.

If you have an SIT you can receive psychotherapeutic, group or individual treatment. There are several therapies that have shown good results in SIT. Some examples are behavioral dialectic therapy, mentalization-based therapy and schema therapy. You could also receive drug treatment.

You also have the right to receive information about existing treatment alternatives and to actively participate in the treatment. It is important that you feel motivated and have confidence in the trafficker.

If you have previously sought assistance, but consider that it did not work, you should not give up, you should seek help again. Research has shown that what determines the success of the treatment is not the type of therapy, but the relationship of trust established with the trafficker

It is not uncommon for you to have other diagnoses besides TIE, for example, ADHD or bipolar disorder. As with the other diagnoses, life improves with time, as you understand yourself better and dare to tell your environment what you need to feel better.

PANIC DISORDER

If you have repeated panic attacks and are worried about finding yourself in situations where you risk suffering a new panic attack, you may have what is called panic disorder. Do not hesitate to ask for help if this is your reality. There are treatments to combat the panic disorder.

What is a panic disorder?

When anxiety comes suddenly and without warning, and feels strongly in the body, it is called panic distress. Typically, panic distress is to believe that there is a physical problem and not a psychological one.

Panic distress is particularly common in situations where there is a sense of confinement, where there is no escape. It could be, for example, when one is in a queue, or sitting on a train or a bus.

The feeling of panic distress is strong in the body and can give rise to symptoms such as palpitations, asphyxiation, and dizziness. Given its strong body presence, it can be difficult to understand that it is a psychological reaction. Instead, it is common to think that there is a physical problem, such as a heart attack. Body reactions are the result of the reaction of your nervous system to a situation that is interpreted as a threat.

If you have repeated panic attacks, it could be a panic disorder. If you have panic distress occasionally, it does not mean you have panic disorder.

How does it affect your life?

If you have panic disorder, you live with such a strong fear of suffering panic distress, which ends up affecting your day today. The fear of suffering from anxiety is called anticipatory anxiety. The more anticipatory anxiety you present, the more it can affect and limit your life.

It could be, for example, that you begin to avoid crowds or travel by underground train or bus, for fear of finding yourself in a place where you may have difficulty getting out.

Avoiding complicated situations can be a short-term relief, but the long-term anxiety worsens. The more space you give to anxiety, the less space is left to live the life you might want to live.

When should I seek help?

If anxiety restricts and directs your life, you should not hesitate to seek help. This is also true if you self-medicate with alcohol or tranquilizers to cope with everyday situations.

There are many things you can do to feel better, and the first is to seek medical assistance. If you don't know where to ask for assistance, you can look for an office . If you don't want to be the one asking for medical assistance, ask someone in your environment to contact the assistance.

A treatment could make you feel better. It is common to receive pharmacological treatment in combination with cognitive-behavioral therapy, brief therapy in the form of conversational therapy or Internet therapy. The treatments are intended to teach you how to handle anxiety so that it does not affect and does not restrict your life.

CHAPTER THREE

SOCIAL ANXIETY SYMPTOMS

Social anxiety disorder, or social phobia, is a condition characterized by persistent and excessive shyness. Children with the disorder have an irrational fear of the judgment of others, which can cause them to avoid situations that induce anxiety or else, have intense suffering for that.

Symptom

- Constant fear of being judged. Children with social anxiety disorder often worry "What happens if I do something stupid?" Or "What happens if I say something wrong?"
- Being afraid and avoiding situations that induce anxiety, such as making presentations, meeting new people, going to parties, eating in front of people, etc.
- Panic reactions such as sweating, trembling and shortness of breath
- Suffering or significant impediment during socialization or at school

Anxiety is an everyday word that is used as a medical term. Anxiety is a dynamic state of the body. It does not persist over time, but changes in different circumstances.

Anxiety is genetically inherent in humans. There is a reason for the evolutionary attachment of anxiety and it is the preparation of the organism for changes in the environment and easier adaptation to them.

During the state of anxiety, specific neuronal systems are activated in the brain. Some of them cause vegetative symptoms such as palpitations, sweating, feeling of suffocation, redness and more. In this order of thought, anxiety is not only a state of the psyche but of the whole organism. It can be said that there is no anxiety without bodily symptoms.

Social anxiety syndrome is the most common anxiety disorder. According to some studies, such a disorder in the United States is about 13%. About half of them unlock it by the age of 10 and the rest by the age of 20.

The syndrome is disabling, with rare remissions. Only 25% of those affected are fully recovered. The syndrome is expressed through fear in social situations in which the person is exposed to the attention of others. The individual is convinced that he or she is an object of interest and that he/she cannot cope with this tension and his / her expectations. The main symptoms are a feeling of overwhelming shame, flushing, shaking, vomiting and urging to urinate.

At first glance, provoking situations may be quite harmless. These could be a telephone conversation, an authority meeting in an area, an overcrowded room entry, or a public transportation vehicle. The syndrome can be expressed as an inability to communicate, an inability to work with other people in one room, or a strong reluctance of the person to see and speak with people at all.

These symptoms break the life trajectory of these people. They are low or not at all socially integrated, have difficulty finding a job and a partner in life. A large proportion of patients with severe forms of the syndrome abuse alcohol.

The sad thing is that these patients can be helped, but it is difficult to understand for them and their loved ones. Social anxiety syndrome is alleviated and treated with antidepressants that affect serotonin levels in the brain.

There are many reasons not to seek medical help. Narrowness is often considered a normal quality, and people are convinced that there is hardly an effective cure for such pathology. On the other hand, there is a stigma attached to mental illness in public opinion. This leads to the reluctance of the patient and his or her relatives to acknowledge the problem before themselves and seek help because they would be branded as "crazy."

There are different nuances in the manifestation of social anxiety syndrome. In some people, it manifests itself as the so-called. pre-stage (or stage) fever. This is the lightest form. However, in no small part, the disease is at its fullest and they are highly socially isolated, deeply disturbed and unhappy.

The approach to such patients requires careful treatment. They do not always assist the doctor in regular appointments because of their increased anxiety. Therefore, they should be calmly and concernedly explained that their condition is understandable to the physician and treatable.

Up to a point, social anxiety or social phobia is a normal and useful emotion, as it motivates people to act more appropriately in specific interpersonal situations (for example, to make a good impression in a job interview, to a person who we find it attractive, etc.). It is very common for people to get nervous in certain social situations, especially when they have to speak in public. However, when a person

suffers from a social anxiety disorder (or social phobia), he feels enormous discomfort and his experience is much more serious, disturbing and disabling.

The social phobia consists of a very marked fear of situations in which the person believes that he can be evaluated or observed by other people and in which he fears to behave in a ridiculous or humiliating way in front of those people or that his anxiety symptoms are noticed. She thinks that the evaluation of others is likely to be negative and harmful to her. This anxiety does not diminish even though you have to continually expose yourself to social situations in your daily life. It is also frequent that anticipatory anxiety occurs, that is, that the person worries long before the feared situation takes place (often daily and for weeks).

The situations that a person with social phobia can fear can be very varied: speaking in public, taking some action in front of other people (eating, writing, reading, etc.), initiating and holding conversations (with strangers, with people outside the circle intimate, etc.), go to parties and social events, be observed when entering a place (for example, a cafeteria), talk with authority figures (teachers, bosses, etc.), be with a person for whom you feel attraction, talk on the phone, use a public restroom, etc.

At the physiological level, there may be an increase in the heart rate, stomach discomfort, dizziness, etc., although the most common symptoms are flushing, trembling and sweating. Many people feel a strong and disabling fear that others will realize these symptoms and "think badly" of them (negative evaluation), being able to develop a specific social phobia, such as erythrophobia (fear of blushing).

At the level of behavior, some avoid the feared social situations, while other people face them but usually resort to using "safety behaviors", that is, behaviors with which they try to protect themselves in one way or another, for example, looking away If you think someone is going to ask you something, support your hands somewhere in case they tremble, put on thick clothes so you feel less sweat.

As for the thoughts, they have usually related to the "certainty" that their way of acting is or will be deficient, that a negative evaluation will occur, and about the "catastrophic" consequences that this will have. Typical thoughts are: "I have made it fatal, I am an idiot, they do not like anything, I am worthless, they will think that I am silly, nobody will want to be with me, I will always be alone", etc.

Although both fear and avoidance can manifest themselves in many different ways, they limit the possibilities of personal development and affect the quality of life in general. The person suffering from this disorder may not be involved in friendship or couple relationships, not promoting themselves in their work or studies, isolating themselves from any social encounter, etc.

AN EXPLANATORY MODEL: WHY DOES SOCIAL PHOBIA OCCUR?

The person with social anxiety perceives social situations as dangerous since they are always running the risk of being rejected, losing status or of not reaching the valuation and status that they want and need. This person wants to be accepted and highly valued, but doubts being able to achieve it. It is perceived as inferior to the others and fears not only the negative assessment (with the consequent damage that could entail) but also that it is not as positive as she needs and constantly tries to prevent it by all means.

When a person with social anxiety anticipates or faces a feared social situation, many alarm signals are activated in their brain and confronts them in a defensive manner. Your resources focus on the threat. On the one hand, it looks for threats from internal sources, that is, it becomes very aware of itself, it observes and uses that information to judge the impression it is causing on others ("my hands shake, then they will think that I am weak and moron"). But on the other hand, it also focuses its attention on threats that might come from abroad (for example, gestures of rejection or boredom that may involve negative assessment).

When these people find themselves in social situations they make comparisons between the impression they want to give (what they think is expected of it) and the way they think they are acting (which they use to draw conclusions about how they think others perceive them). For example: "I should speak fluently, be witty and pleasant, but I am anxious, my voice trembles and I am doing it fatal so that others will believe that I am incompetent or silly."

If you can avoid the social situation and if this is impossible, you will use the "safety behaviors". Thus, the person is trapped in a vicious circle where he obtains evidence of his previous assumptions and there is no opportunity to prove that such fears are unfounded.

FACTORS THAT CONTRIBUTE TO A PERSON BEING VULNERABLE TO SOCIAL PHOBIA

a) Rigid rules. Some people have rigid and over-perfectionist rules that govern their social behavior, such as "I must always have something interesting to say," "I must always be witty and fluently verbal," "I should never show signs of anxiety." These people can function normally until a major failure occurs when these self-demands are not met. Afterward, social situations are perceived as dangerous, since they can lead to other failures.

b) Dysfunctional assumptions. They refer to the catastrophic consequences of behaving in a certain way: "If I am silent they will think that I am bored", "If they see that I tremble they will think that I am stupid", "If they see me anxious they will think that I am incompetent". At the same time, they evaluate the occurrence of these evaluations as something terrible: "it would be terrible to be considered bored or incompetent; that would show how little I am worth, I would be left alone," etc.

c) Negative beliefs about himself. They are beliefs that focus on oneself and are activated in social situations, that is, they would not be chronically activated (I am stupid, I am bored, I am worthless, I am not interesting; etc.). When the person is not in situations that cause anxiety, these beliefs are less credible, but they are easily activated as soon as a social stressor occurs. Schemes of this type make the individual more likely to assess the social situation as dangerous because he could "prove" that those beliefs are true, which would be "terrible."

CHAPTER FOUR

DEFEAT SOCIAL PHOBIA WITHOUT A PSYCHOLOGIST

Social phobia is a disorder that can cause us great discomfort. Shame, fear and sensitivity unite , creating a dangerous cocktail. We can differentiate the symptoms that social phobia produces in two types according to their nature:

Physical symptoms

- Nausea and stomach aches.
- Tremors and even tachycardias.
- Uncontrollable sweats
- Dizziness, lightheadedness and, in extreme cases, fainting.
- Stuttering or other speech difficulties.

Psychological symptoms

- Afraid to say something and be ridiculous for their opinions or feelings.

- Concern for social events days and weeks before they occur.
- Irrational fear of making a mistake and being judged by others.
- Alcohol consumption to relax the other physical or psychological symptoms.
- Hypersensitivity to any comments from unknown people or even close friends.
- Avoidance and fear of public spaces.
- I refuse to meet new people or perform different activities.

If we recognize more than one symptom of the aforementioned and these are a problem for us to lead a normal life, we may be suffering from social phobia. In this case, we need to have the best tools to overcome this mental condition.

Anxiety or social phobia

The origin of social phobia is something very studied by the community of psychologists. Anxiety or social phobia can have many causes, it can arise from a traumatic event or it can develop throughout our lives. Some psychologists argue that social anxiety has a strong genetic influence. Other scholars defend the theory of learning: if from a young age they teach us to be afraid, we will be afraid of everything around us.

Over the years, after much debate, it has been concluded that social phobia is a disorder with many causes and variables that interact with each other. Next, we will point out the most common variables:

Psychological variables

We understand as psychological variables those that occur in our mind and are part of our way of thinking. A cause of social phobia can be the ability to interact with other people, if we are not very good, we can feel fear in the next social interactions. Our education of children or adolescents also greatly influences the emergence of social anxiety: overprotective parents may not give us the best tools to handle us fluently in the environment and create fear of the unknown.

Biological or neurological variables

In this case, we talk about a physical influence on the emergence of social phobia. It has been scientifically proven that a high level of serotonin (the happiness hormone) can be one of the causes of the appearance of this disorder. Genetic causes have also been studied, they state that if our parents have social phobia, we will be more likely to suffer from it.

Whatever the origin, we must admit that anxiety or social phobia is an unpleasant condition with terrible consequences in our body. It can create traumas, general anxiety, respiratory or heart problems. Therefore, we must act as effectively as possible to eradicate it.

HOW TO OVERCOME SOCIAL PHOBIA

To overcome social phobia without a psychologist, it is necessary to have very clear objectives and focus on them. We must go step by step, training our body and mind to not feel fear in any situation. In order to cure this malaise, we suggest a series of self-help tips and strategies:

Your thoughts are valid: recognizing the value of what we think can help us improve our self-esteem. In this way, we will increase self-confidence and dare to express what we think to other people.

Develop your full potential: each person is different and has different abilities from others. We should not feel less about not having the same social skills as other people, accepting ourselves as we are will be the most important step. Subsequently, we can fully exploit our capabilities and thus increase our self-esteem.

Being reflective is a positive thing: the most introverted people are usually reflexive, this can lead us to have ideas or reach conclusions that nobody else had raised. If we share our reflections to the world, it will thank us, we have much to contribute and little to fear.

Train your social skills: once our self-esteem and safety have improved, it is time to put our skills into practice. To do this, it is better to do it step by step, going to small social gatherings or talking with a closed circle of friends is a good start. Little by little, we can go further to end up going to events that we would never have imagined going.

Social phobia: drug treatment and natural remedies

To accompany the coping strategies mentioned above, we can resort to other treatments, both natural and pharmacological remedies. These work as a helpful tool to relax anxiety symptoms, but they don't cure the disorder. If you need a pharmacological treatment, it is essential to consult with an expert before. Self-medication is something that should be avoided since we do not control the effects that drugs have on our bodies.

Anxiolytics

These are the main medications to reduce anxiety symptoms. They relax our muscles, decrease heartbeats and help us fall asleep. Among the best-known anxiolytics, we highlight Lorazepam, Bromazepam, and Diazepam.

It should be noted that we should not take antidepressants if we suffer from anxiety or social phobia. It turns out that if we have this disorder, we produce too much serotonin, so taking antidepressants would only make the problem worse.

Valerian

Valerian root is a known natural remedy to cure all kinds of anxiety or nervousness. This can be taken as a tea or from an extract. Valerian has relaxing and sedative effects that reduce the symptoms of social phobia, this helps us to better manage our emotions and, thus, try to improve social skills.

Meditation

Meditation combined with breathing exercises is a good treatment to relieve our nervousness. Learning to relax the body only by controlling it from within, prevents us from creating dependence on other drugs or substances.

HOW TO OVERCOME DEPRESSION BY LONELINESS

The pain of depression by loneliness does not heal in a day. Nor in a week. However, with a few simple changes in your attitude to the present, you can open a new door of hope. How to feel more accompanied? Keep reading and here you will find some good tips.

- Search occupations. Being busy is very important to stop that inertia of turning so many heads. Courses, conferences, reading books and magazines, running errands, housework, plans ... The best way to have a day with homework is to establish a predictable routine. This routine helps you gain mental strength from everyday life.

- Plans that bring your company. There are some plans that, although you make them alone, give you company as a side effect. For example, cinema, literature, walks in the park, visiting museums, writing a newspaper, making word searches or crossword puzzles ...

- Take care. A routine as daily as going to the hairdresser can have a totally emotional value for those who look in the mirror with the feeling of a new look. A makeover can be an anchor to start a new stage. Likewise, a shopping session to update the basics of the wardrobe with a trend of the season, allows you to pamper yourself as you deserve. Sometimes, loneliness leads to one's own neglect of personal image.

- Psychological help. When a person suffers from depression, he needs to ask for help. A person who feels lonely suffers even more because he feels he only counts on himself to break this pain inertia. However, a psychological therapy allows you to receive therapeutic advice from an expert who, with his presence, reminds you that you are not alone. There are also other forms of help. For example, participation in personal growth courses. Similarly, there are emotional support entities. For example, the Telephone of Hope answers calls from people with their own history. Some of those stories have to do with loneliness.

- Socialization spaces. The feeling of loneliness increases when you stay most of the time between the four walls of your home. You can read books at home. However, you can also do it in your neighborhood library or in a cafeteria you like. But the feeling you will have is very different. You will see other people. And this is very positive.

- Voluntary activity. If you value the idea of volunteering, it is very important that you choose an activity that you like and enjoy. An activity that makes you feel good. Sometimes, volunteering is therapeutic because it helps us forget ourselves to focus on external aspects.

- Social networks. Social networks do not cover the emotional deficiencies that a human being has. However, it is important not to minimize the value that new forms of communication have in the life of a human being. Through social networks you can interact with people who live far away, you can be informed of interesting topics and you feel connected with others.

- Promote personal relationships at work. Many friendly ties arise in the office. And, in addition, even though many of these ties remain only in the workplace, these relationships are very constructive for your self-esteem. And, of course, they also bring you company during your working time.

- Dance lessons. Dance classes can be very therapeutic because they combine music and body movement. But, in addition, in this fun space, you can meet new people.
- Cry when you need it but don't pity your situation. Think simply that this will also happen. Especially, if you take some actions to change your situation.

Do you have a bad time at social events, do you feel you do not fit or do you feel inferior when you are with other people you do not know? Do you feel a bitter fear of rejection or criticism? Extreme shame to be with strangers? The truth is that one thing is shyness or having a more introverted or reserved personality (I am in that group), but another very different is really suffering and having a bad time because of shame to the point of needing to hide or run away from certain situations. If so - if it is your case or that of someone you know, very possibly this article on how to overcome social phobia may come as a ring to your finger.

Social phobia is an irrational fear in situations in which we interact with others. While it is true that it is normal to get nervous at some times (when you have to speak in public, for example) or feel a little out of place with strangers, suffering from anxiety or very high levels of suffering is not something so common or natural, So we will be talking about a social anxiety disorder.

Behind that fear of people hide many others: the fear of being rejected, to be humiliated, to be judged, criticized, to feel inferior ... And most importantly: they all hide one of the greatest fears in society, which is the fear of not being enough.

FEAR OF PEOPLE IS TOTALLY IRRATIONAL AND IMAGINARY

That phobia of people can make us think that everyone is watching us, that everyone is talking behind our backs, criticizing us; an obsession is generated for the fear of being the center of attention. Actually that fear is absurd and irrational, but the body and our emotions do not understand irrational issues. They only know that what our mind thinks and imagines, our body feels and suffers.

The social phobics usually already know that it is an irrational fear, they should not have, but knowing is not enough and in certain situations are unable to control that anxiety and fears.

When a social phobia is severe it is important to carry out a psychological treatment with a professional. Normally for this type of case, Cognitive Behavioral Therapy is used, which will make it easier for them to find out at what time and what was the origin of the problem. In addition, it is perfect to create strategies and find solutions to many cases around phobias.

Get out of yourself

One of the symptoms of social anxiety is that those who suffer from it focus totally on themselves, obsessing with what they will say, what they will think ... The focus is always on them, and what happens is that when they focus more on themselves it is much worse. Therefore, the goal should be to leave oneself, think and be more interested in others, ask, be filled with curiosity to meet those around them ... That will help them not to worry or focus so much on what frightens them and reduce their anxiety levels

Working on your self-acceptance

One of the best keys to overcoming a social phobia? Work on self-esteem, trust, and self-acceptance. All of them are fundamental factors and the reason is clear: if we accept ourselves, if we continue to progress in our level of personal development, if we continue to grow and improve our self-image, many of those fears that cause social phobia will gradually fade away.

The important thing is what you think of yourself, not what others may think. When we have good self-esteem, we do not worry or influence so much what others may think or possible criticisms. Trust and self-acceptance are the pillars that keep us firm in our principles and values, in our beliefs, in our own valuation and respect.

Stop running away

The objective must be to stop fleeing from situations that cause us fear or phobia because fleeing perpetuates fears. When we face them is when we overcome them. Little by little you have to learn to expose yourself to these situations and face them not as threats, but as challenges; turn them into opportunities to overcome and conquer oneself.

Sometimes we worry about what others may think of us, about that fear of being judged or criticized, but the truth is that everyone has enough with their own. And in reality, most of them will be quite busy with their own problems to be thinking about you, so don't think you are important enough to think that everyone focuses on what you say or do.

Control your breathing

This technique serves to reduce tensions of the nervous system . You have several options, but we recommend you to take measures in breathing and exhale slowly through your nose, with your mouth closed.

This method can be carried out anywhere and at any time. Take the time you need and don't feel pressured. It is very important that you do this exercise slowly and with all the repetitions you need.

If you are in a quiet environment and have the possibility of lying down, use a relaxation technique. Relaxation combined with diaphragmatic breathing will certainly reduce suffocating breathing, tachycardia, and tremor.

Being in the midst of a social anxiety attack, the best thing you can do is stay as calm as possible.

Include more fermented foods

Fermented food containing probiotics reduces the permeability of the mucosa of the intestine. Probiotics also decrease inflammation of the intestines.

This is good news since anxiety is often accompanied by gastrointestinal symptoms. Therefore, reducing inflammation helps relieve symptoms.

It is said that fermented foods also help modify the body's response due to stress. And this answer is highly related to mental health disorders, such as social anxiety. In addition, the consumption of fermented milk reduces the brain's responses to facial expressions and negative social stimuli.

Cognitive psychotherapy

Cognitive psychotherapy is a type of treatment that usually has a great effect on the quality of life of people with social anxiety, and that helps reduce their symptoms.

In therapy, the patient learns to control the negative thoughts that he carries with him. This produces an immediate change, as it develops skills that will gain confidence if it is the case.

If you decide to take this kind of therapy constantly you will be exposed to social situations that cause you to fear or reprimand. Facing these types of situations is essential to gain confidence and be able to handle yourself in daily life.

Exercise

The practice of any sport helps to combat social anxiety and its effects because it increases the production of serotonin. This substance increases the feeling of pleasure and will make it easier for you to deal with negative emotions.

Walking three times a week, at least for half an hour, can help with anxiety. The walk can also be used to relax the mind and perform active meditation. When you walk, you think. And being a repetitive movement, you end up working on the points that generate anxiety.

Perhaps you have already enjoyed the benefits of the walk unconsciously. We invite you to do it this time in a totally conscious way. The practice of some sport will also help you interact with others and gradually overcome social anxiety.

Ingest amino acids

To control social anxiety, we can consume banana and chocolate moderately. Both contain tryptophan, an amino acid precursor to serotonin.

Another possibility is to consume tryptophan in capsules together with vitamin B6 and magnesium. Other amino acids that may help are taurine and glutamine. These increase the availability of a neurotransmitter called GABA, which is an organism that physiologically controls anxiety.

We can ingest them in capsules or infusions. Most contain substances that function as mild sedatives that help control anxiety daily.

The plants known and studied with this action are chamomile and valerian.

Medication

If you have already tried everything and you feel that your situation only gets worse, you should make an appointment with a specialist. Although many people completely refuse this option, there are a lot of medications that can help you control social anxiety.

The reuptake inhibitors of serotonin are the primary medication used to treat this disordered behavior. To reduce the risk of side effects, the doctor may begin by prescribing low doses of the medication to be eliminated as symptoms are eliminated.

The treatment can last several weeks or several months but the symptoms will reduce considerably. If you do not want to take medication, you can try the other alternatives. Just remember that this therapy is not bad or a sign that you are crazy. It is only an extra help to be healthy and functional.

Social anxiety: an increasingly common problem

In social phobia, people suffer anxiety crises when they are with other people or in situations where they must spend time with others. Its incidence has been increasing and today causes many people suffering.

This list does not show all the complete treatments to treat this disease. Psychotherapy is a valuable resource to deal with this form of illness.

Social anxiety has several levels and types, so it is necessary to know how to distinguish it from shyness, which is a frequent non-pathological behavior.

CHAPTER FIVE

OVERCOMING SOCIAL ANXIETY

Some people can have serious problems trying to communicate with peers that are associated with feelings of anxiety or fear. If this is something you deal with, you may have a social phobia, also called social anxiety disorder. There are many steps you can take to help you deal more effectively with day to day interactions.

Confronting Social Anxiety Disorder

Confront your negative thoughts. Social anxiety disorder can cause you to think negative thoughts about yourself when faced with a social situation. You may think "I'll look like a fool" or "I'm going to humiliate myself." The first step to overcoming them is to identify the thoughts when they pop into your head. Knowing what is causing social phobia can help you overcome it.

- Stop yourself when you think these thoughts and say, "No, I will not look like a fool. I am strong and competent and I'm going to get through this."

Test the reality of your fear. After you have confronted and identified the thoughts, analyze the fear.

Try to overwrite the negative thoughts in your brain with positive, realistic ones.

- Ask yourself questions about your negative thoughts. For example, ask "Do I know I'm going to humiliate myself" or "How do I know I'm going to blow my presentation?" Then ask yourself, "Will it be the end of the world if I mess up?" The logical answers to the questions are: more than likely, you will not humiliate yourself or mess up. Even if you do mess up, you are human, as is everyone watching you. Even professionals mess up.

Stop unrealistic predictions. One unhelpful thing people do when dealing with social fears is making false, unrealistic predictions about the social situation. You can't predict what will happen. If you try, you will only come up with the worst-case scenario, which will not be close to a realistic reflection of the actual event. This only causes unnecessary anxiety.

- Remember that you have the power to change your exaggerated thoughts. For example, if you're going to a wedding, focus on the fact that you won't be the center of attention.
- Visualize being at the wedding and speaking confidently to others and enjoying yourself.

Realize that not everyone is judging you. Often times social fears can be a result of thinking that everyone around you is passing judgment on you. If so, take a step back, and realize that most people aren't focused on you. If they are focused on you, they are not thinking the same negative thoughts as you are.

- Don't try to read people's minds. You can't know what people are thinking. Plus, they do not see the same negative self that you see in your mind.
- Use social situations to practice changing negative thoughts about yourself, and practice stopping and altering your thoughts about judgment from others.

Understand that everyone feels anxiety. You are not the only person that feels anxiety in social situations. Over 12% of the population has it, and that number is increasing.

- Understanding this can help put you on the same level as everyone around you. You are not alone in your fears. Also, since everyone feels anxiety from time to time, remembering this can help you realize people won't criticize or judge you if they realize you are anxious.

Understand overcoming this will take practice. Overcoming your social anxiety won't happen overnight. It takes commitment and lots of practice. You are learning new behaviors, new patterns of thinking, and new social skills. This all takes practice. However, little by little, you will learn these new skills and start being able to overcome or manage your phobia.

Change your focus. One of the ways to help reduce your anxiety is to take the focus off of yourself in social situations. Try to pay attention to your surroundings, the conversation, and connecting with the people around you.

- Begin to understand that although you are focused on how others will think of you, everyone else is not as focused on you. If you say or do something embarrassing, others may not even notice. Or if they do, they will quickly forget it.
- Try to focus on other things when you notice your physical symptoms in social situations. You are not being as obvious as you think. It is very rare that others can notice physical symptoms of anxiety or even panic attacks. Instead notice your experiences of the event, such as music you hear, how each bite of food tastes, or other entertainment such as art or dancing.
- Most people are just as nervous in social situations as you are. They are too busy focused on themselves.

Working on Your Fears

Take gradual steps. Make a list of 10 situations that cause you anxiety. Rank them, placing the most stressful at the top. Starting at the bottom, try to gradually face each anxiety-inducing situation.

- Wait until you feel moderately comfortable with the previous situation before moving to the more stressful one. You want to overcome your anxiety, not increase it.

- This list may take a while to get through, and that's okay. You may never reach number 10. But if you have conquered 1-7, you have made your social phobia significantly more manageable.
- If you feel you are struggling through this, contact a mental health professional who can offer you support while you attempt to face each fear on your list.

Make observable goals for yourself. Getting over your social anxiety may seem like a nebulous process. How do you know if you are getting better? Just putting yourself in social situations isn't enough. That might be step 1, but after that, you need to work on interacting more. Make goals for yourself for each social outing. As you accomplish your goals, you can start to see progress and improvement in yourself.

- Make small talk with people you see often, such as employees, schoolmates, or other people that you come in contact with. This may be just a comment on the weather, your homework or work project, or the meeting you had earlier. Start by giving yourself a goal of speaking to one person once a week. Then increase it to every day, or speaking to multiple people in one day.
- Make a goal to make one comment in class or in your meeting. Don't worry about what everyone

else thinks. Focus on the fact that you did it. That is progress.

- If you are in a group setting, make a pact with yourself to say at least 3 comments in the conversation.
- Ask someone to dinner. It can be as a friend or as a date. Don't focus on the response - only focus on the fact that you were assertive and asked.
- This helps you focus on the task and the goal, not the nerves. The idea here is to get control of the situation. You know you can control what you do, what you say, and what you ask. You can't control the other person, so don't worry about them.
- You can even try practicing with a friend at home what you'll do or say in social situations.

Relax. Try to program yourself to stop worrying about social situations. Instead, relax. Worrying and stressing about the event causes you to have anxiety when you finally get to the situation.

- Try thinking about the event while you are relaxed. Take a warm bath, curl up in a cozy blanket, or listen to your favorite song. Think about the upcoming event. Since you are in a good, relaxed headspace, this can help you feel better about the upcoming event.
- Imagine that you are in the situation. Imagine yourself relaxed and confident. Thinking about the situation in a positive, relaxed way can help you overcome negative thoughts.

Practice deep breathing. Deep breathing can be a great way to manage anxiety during or before social situations. Deep breathing can help reduce the physical symptoms of your anxiety, many of which are a result of breathing too quickly. Do breathing exercises every day so it becomes second nature and comes naturally when you're in a stressful situation.

- Breathe through your abdomen, not your chest. To do this, lay on the floor or sit straight in a chair. Place a hand on your chest, the other on your abdomen. As you inhale, the hand on your abdomen should move while the one on your chest stays mostly at the same place.
- Inhale slowly and deeply through your nose. Hold for a count of 7. Exhale slowly through your mouth for a count of 8. Gently contract your abdominal muscles to get all the air from the lungs. This is extremely important.
- Complete 5 deep breaths. Try 1 deep breath per 10 seconds.

Find support from friends and family. Talking to family and friends about your problems is extremely important. A good friend or family member will help to motivate you and help you overcome your fear. Ask these people to help support you as you gain the courage to try something new.

- Ask your family or friends to go places with you that cause anxiety. Sometimes going to new places with someone you trust can help reduce your anxiety.

- Make sure you lean on supportive, positive, and encouraging friends and family members. If they are negative, put you down, lecture you, or criticize you, find someone else to support you.

Interacting in Social Situations

Socialize more. Although you may be terrified of putting yourself in social situations, you should seek out social situations. The more you avoid something, the more control it has over your mind. The anxiety around it will grow until it becomes something you fear. The more you get used to something, the less fear and control it has over you.

- Try making spaces yours. Anything is nerve-wracking when it's unfamiliar. Go to a restaurant, a part of town, or your gym. Walk around. Become familiar with it. Once you start to become familiar with a place, it can feel more comfortable. Plus, you start to put your focus on your surroundings. Then you can start socializing with people.
- Take someone with you. You don't have to do this alone. Take a friend or family member to an event. Start small. Take a free class at a community center, go to a group class at the gym, volunteer, or join a meetup group and attend a gathering.

Find a club, team, or a group that relates to one of your interests and skills. Finding people with similar interests can help you interact with people. Clubs and groups may give you a smaller environment to socialize in, which may help your anxiety. This makes it easier to force yourself to talk because you can't just get lost in the crowd.

Concentrate on the conversation. When you are in a social situation, try concentrating on the conversation instead of your own anxieties. This helps you connect with other people, which is a good thing, and offers you opportunities to talk. When you start to worry about how you look to everyone else, pause and refocus on the present moment. Add comments and talk when it seems natural.

- Focus on the present, instead of replaying things that have already happened.

Try to tough it out. When you are in a situation that causes you anxiety, try to hang in there. At first, the anxiety may feel unbearable, but anxiety gradually lessens the longer you are in a situation. Try to stay in the situation until your anxiety reduces by half. This may take up to half an hour, but oftentimes it lessens quickly.

Some social situations are quick, like saying hello or making small talk. Although that may cause anxiety that you can't wait though, you can feel good about speaking to the person and making small talk.

Observe and listen when in large groups. Large group situations are great places to practice. You can socialize and be around other people without being the center of attention. There are a bunch of people contributing to the conversation, so don't feel like you're pressured to say something. Try to be comfortable. Look around at the other people in the room. Are they all focused on you? Or are they enjoying everyone's company?

- When you get a chance to contribute something meaningful that you think the others will appreciate, throw it in there. You'll do just fine.
- This is a great place to make goals for yourself. Start by saying you'll say one thing in the conversation, and increase as you get more comfortable.

Remember that most people don't focus on your flaws. Most people don't pay attention to people's flaws. Most people make an effort to pay attention to the good things people do and say. Feel confident in this knowledge and express your good qualities. Be yourself. Most people will enjoy your company.

- Those who pick at your flaws usually do so because of a lack of self-esteem on their part. If they are judging you, you don't want to be around them in the first place.

Be friendly and kind. People like to be around people who make them happy, and kindness is a really easy way to make others happy. Give genuine compliments, make eye contact, show interest, and smile. Whatever you can do to brighten someone's day is a point in your favor.

Getting Help

See your doctor. If you believe you have social anxiety, go see your doctor. Many doctors will work with you to make your visit as easy and anxiety-free as possible. Some may discuss your condition with you over the phone, while others may give you an appointment time before or after business hours. Speak with your doctor so you can start taking steps to help your phobia.

Try therapy. If your social anxiety is too bad to manage on your own, consult a professional. Therapy may be key to overcoming social anxiety. A therapist can help you with Cognitive Behavior Therapy (CBT), which teaches you a different way of thinking, behaving, and reacting to social situations. It can help you feel less anxious and fearful.

- CBT helps you learn how to manage physical symptoms through relaxation and breathing, replace negative thoughts with more balanced ones, and gradually face social situations.

Take part in group therapy. In group therapy situations, you undergo CBT in a group setting. This includes role-playing, social skills training, acting, videotaping, and mock interviews. These exercises are supposed to help you face situations that would make you anxious in the real world and prepare for them.

Join a support group. A support group is different than group therapy because it's aimed at helping you gain the support you need during your recovery. Support groups can help you not feel isolated from your anxiety. You can look for support groups in your areas.

Use medication. Sometimes medication can be used to help with the symptoms of social anxiety, but medicine will not cure it. As soon as you stop the medication, symptoms such as anxiety will return. Medicine is generally used alongside therapy and self-help techniques.

- Common medications used are Beta-blockers for performance anxiety that help the physical symptoms of anxiety, antidepressants, and benzodiazepines.

CHAPTER SIX

HOW TO OVERCOME SHYNESS

Are you shy? If so, you are far from alone. Many people in the world suffer from mild to extreme shyness and are struggling to overcome it. To overcome shyness, you'll need to understand the circumstances that trigger your shyness, work to change your mental state and perspective regarding those circumstances, and practice putting yourself in comfortable and uncomfortable situations until you've worked through the worries holding you back. Remember that breaking out of your shell doesn't magically happen overnight. It takes time, effort, and of course, the desire to change.

Think about the root of your shyness. Shyness doesn't necessarily equate to being introverted or not liking yourself. It simply means that for some reason you get embarrassed when the spotlight hits you. What's the root of your shyness? It's generally the symptom of a larger problem. Here are four possibilities:

- You have a weak self-image. This happens when we evaluate ourselves and that voice in our heads is negative. It's tough to stop listening to it, but at the end of the day it's your voice and you can tell it what to say.

- You have issues believing compliments given to you. Whether or not you think you look good, someone did, and that's why they told you so. You wouldn't call them a liar, would you? Lift your chin, say "thank you" and accept it. Don't try to tell the person who paid you a compliment that they're wrong.

- You are preoccupied with how you come off. This happens when we focus too much on ourselves. Because we spend all day monitoring our actions and making sure we don't mess up, we assume everyone else is too. We'll talk about turning the focus on others if this sounds like you.

- You are labeled as shy by others. Sometimes, when we're little, we're shy. Unfortunately, people latch onto that and treat us as such, even when our personalities grow out of it. It's possible that others have lumped you into this category and you're trying to accommodate them. The good news? You only have to accommodate yourself.

Whatever your reason, it's doable to get over it. They're all ways of thinking and thinking is the one thing you have control over. Yes!

Accept your shyness. One of the first steps to overcome your shyness is to try to accept your shyness and be comfortable with it. The more you will resist it unconsciously or consciously, the longer it will prevail. If you are shy then accept it and embrace it totally. One way it could be done is by saying to yourself repeatedly 'Yes I am shy and I accept it'.

Figure out your triggers. Do you become shy in front of new audiences? When learning a new skill? When venturing into a new situation? When surrounded by people you know and admire? When you don't know anyone somewhere? Try to pinpoint the thoughts that go through your head right before the shyness hits.

Odds are not all situations that make you shy. You're okay being around your family, right? How are they that different than the strangers around you? They're not -- you just know them better and what's more, they know you. It's not you, it's just the situations you're in. This proves that it's not a global, 100% of-the-time thing. Excellent.

Make a list of situations that make you feel anxious. Order them so that those things that cause you the least anxiety are first and those that cause you the most anxiety are last. When you put things in concrete terms, it feels like a task you can tackle and tackle successfully.

- Make them as concrete as possible. "Talking in front of people" may be a trigger, but you can get more specific. Talking in front of those who have more authority than you do? Talking to those you find attractive? The more specific you are, the easier it will be to identify the situation and work through it.

Conquer the list. Once you have a list of 10-15 stressful situations, start working through them, one-by-one (after you read the article, of course). The first few "easier" situations will help build your confidence so that you can continue moving to more difficult situations on your list.

Don't worry if you have to go backward on the list sometimes; take it at your own pace, but make an effort to push yourself.

Conquering Your Mind

Use this shyness as a Cue. Whatever inside you that triggers shyness is because we perceive it as a trigger for shyness. It's like computer programming when in a 'program' gets a certain type to interrupt it behaves in the same way how we have programmed it to handle interrupts. Similarly, our mind can be programmed too. In a way, we were programmed since our childhood, to react to certain stimuli like stay away from strangers, heights, dangerous animals, etc. We often react automatically, reacting in a way that comes naturally to us (by default) and this reaction could be flawed. For example: when people see a lizard some see an ugly reptile, while others would perceive a beautiful pet. This difference comes from their memories and experiences (or lack of experience) with the stimuli (lizard). In the same way, when shy people see people(stimuli) your natural response is shyness. The truth is that you can change this response by re-programming your mind. Some ways this could be done by...

Questioning yourself and checking the validity of your reasons. For example, it's essential that you practice speaking in public to really overcome the problem of shyness. Try to see this shyness as a cue to push yourself hard and to do the opposite of what you have been doing when you feel shy. When you feel shy in public, you probably leave for a quiet place because this has been your default reaction for so long. But this time when you feel shy, push yourself and do the opposite; i.e., talk to people. Yes, you will feel extremely uncomfortable but again see these emotions as a trigger to push yourself even harder. The greater the magnitude of these negative emotions, the harder they will motivate you to push yourself. After trying this for several times you will realize that these negative feelings and emotions were actually your good friends because they motivated you to push yourself even harder.

Place your attention on others. For 99% of us, we become shy when we think if we speak up or stand out, we'll embarrass ourselves. That's why it's important to focus on others, placing our (mental) attention elsewhere. When we stop focusing on ourselves, we stop being able to be worried about how we come off.

The easiest way to do this is to concentrate on compassion.[5] When we're feeling compassionate, sympathetic, or even empathetic, we stop being concerned about ourselves and start devoting all our mental resources to understanding others. Remembering that everyone is fighting some sort of battle -- big or small (big to them!) -- helps us remember everyone deserves our care.

If that doesn't work, imagine a thinking pattern like you imagine other people have. If you're worried about how you look, you're assuming everyone else is outwardly focused (hint: they're actually not). Thinking patterns are contagious; once you start, you won't be able to stop.

Visualize success. Close your eyes and visualize a situation where you might be shy. Now, in your mind's eye, think about being confident. Do this often, and for different situations. This is most effective if you do this daily, especially in the morning. It might feel silly, but athletes use visualization to develop their skills, so why not you?

Involve all your senses to make it feel the most real. Think about being happy and comfortable. What do you sound like? What are you doing? That way when the time comes, you'll be prepared.

Practice good posture. Standing tall gives the world the impression that you are self-confident and receptive to others. Often we are treated the way we feel -- so if you feel open and approachable, your body will emulate that feeling. Body over matter!

This will fool your brain, too. Research says that good posture (head held high, shoulders back, and open arms) makes us feel authoritative, confident, and -- to top it off -- reduces stress. And you didn't even need more reasons!

Practice speaking clearly to yourself. This will help avoid the potential embarrassment of needing to repeat what you said due to mumbling or talking too quietly. You gotta get used to hearing your own voice! Loving it, even.

Record yourself pretending to have conversations. Sounds ridiculous, sure, but you'll notice patterns, when and why you drop off, times when you assume you're speaking loudly but you're really not, etc. In the beginning, you'll feel like an actor (and do things actors do to get in the moment), but it will become an old habit. Practice makes habits, you know!

Don't compare yourself to others. The more you compare yourself to others, the more you will feel that you are not able to measure up and the more intimidated you will feel, which will make you shyer. There is no use to compare yourself to anybody else -- but if you do, do it realistically. Everyone else is overwrought with self-assurance problems, too!

Think about how gosh darn great you are. Everyone has some special gifts or traits to offer to the world. It may sound corny, but it's true. Think about what you know, what you can do, and what you have accomplished, rather than fixating on how you look, sound, or dress. Keep in mind that everyone, even the "beautiful people," has something about themselves or their life that they don't like. There's no particular reason why your "problem" should make you shy while their "problem" doesn't make them shy.

When you concentrate on this, you'll realize you have plenty to offer any group or situation. Your resources and skills are needed to improve any issue, conversation, or circumstance. Knowing this, you'll feel more inclined to speak up.

Identify your social values and strengths. Just because you're not the alpha in the room, have the most booming voice, or get the party started doesn't mean you lack social strengths. Are you a great listener? Do you have an eye for detail? It's possible it's something that's not even occurred to you, so sit back for a second. Are you better at observing than most of those around you? Probably.

Your strengths can give you an advantage. If you're a great listener, you'll probably be able to see when someone has a problem and needs to vent a little. In this circumstance, they are the one that needs you. There's nothing threatening about that situation. So ask them what's up! You noticed they're steaming at the ears a little bit -- can you lend an ear of yours?

In every social group, all the roles need to be filled. You have a place even if you don't see it. None is better than any other -- know that your value, whatever it may be, completes the group dynamic.

Don't get caught up in labels. For the record, popular people aren't happy. Extroverts aren't necessarily popular or happy and shy people aren't necessarily introverts, unhappy, or cold and aloof. Just as you don't want to be caught up in labels, don't tack them onto anyone else either.

The popular kids at school are trying super hard, day in and day out, to be popular. They're trying to conform and fit in and succeed. Good on them, but it doesn't mean they're happy or that it'll last. Trying to emulate something that isn't as it seems won't get you anywhere. You're better off going to the beat of your own drum -- the high school drum ends, the college drum ends, and then what would you be left with? A couple of drumsticks and a funny hat.

Conquering Social Situations

Get informed. If you're attending a party next week, it's a good idea to prepare yourself with a couple of hot topics. Is the government shutting down again? A hot TV show finale? An international event? Read up. That way when the topic comes up in conversation, you'll be able to chip in.

You're not looking to impress here with your thorough and in-depth knowledge. You're simply looking to join in.

Others aren't looking to be judged or be handed opinions, so keep it light and friendly. A simple, "Man, I wouldn't want to be in Boehner's shoes" can keep the conversation from hitting a standstill.

Think of conversations in stages. Social interaction can be simplified, to a point. When you get down the basic steps and internalize them, you'll be ready to go about conversations on autopilot, which is a lot less stressful. Think about all conversations in four stages:

- Stage one is a simple opening line. It's the small talk at its finest.
- Stage two is the introductions. Self-explanatory.
- Stage three is finding some common ground, some topics you can both talk about.
- Stage four is closing, one party informing the other of their departure, and summing up, possibly exchanging information. "Well, it was great talking to you -- I never thought about Walt that way. Here's my card -- let's chat again soon!"

Start a conversation. Remember that awesome project you completed? That mountain you hiked up? That illness you overcame? If you can do all those things, this conversation will be a piece of cake. A random comment about something you two share will start it off -- "This dang bus is always late," or "Just gotta have faith that the coffee is coming!" or "Did you see Mr. Bossman's tie today? Ho. Ly. Cow." They'll take it from there.

Add detail to basic statements. If someone asks you where you live, it's easy for the conversation to stop in a super-awkward, feel-like-you've-failed dead halt. Instead of saying "On Jump Street," say, "On Jump Street, right next to that awesome bakery. That way, the person has something to comment on, keeping the conversation going. Instead of replying, "Oh, cool." They'll say, "Ohmigod, have you tried their chocolate croissants?!"

Warm-up. If you're at a party, you can have the same exact conversation over and over and over. Hit up one or two people at a time and practice the same social pleasantries and platitudes until you've got it and are practically nauseated. Then move back to the people you really enjoyed talking to. You can zero in on a real conversation then.

Start off quickly, each conversation only lasting a few minutes. This will take the pressure off you and probably make you less nervous -- when the end is 120 seconds away, it's not that scary. Then you can focus your time and energy on those you'd like to be friends with. Really, it makes the most sense for your time and resources.

Look and act approachable. Convey an open, friendly attitude with your body language. Make sure to keep your arms uncrossed, your head up, and your hands not preoccupied. No one will talk to you if you're buried in a game of Candy Crush. They're just being polite!

Think of the people you would want to approach. What do their bodies and faces say? Now think of the people you wouldn't want to approach. How you're sitting right now -- where does it fall on the spectrum?

Smile and make eye contact. A simple smile in the direction of a stranger may brighten your day, and it will brighten theirs too! Smiling is a friendly way to acknowledge others, and it makes a pretty good lead-in to start a conversation with anyone, stranger or friend. You're showing you're harmless, friendly, and wanting to engage.

Humans are social creatures. A simple look at prisoners in solitary confinement will prove that. All of us are seeking interaction and reaffirmation. You're not imposing on their day -- you're making it more vibrant and, well, better.

Think about your body. When you're in a group of people (or even just one person), you'll probably get caught up in some shy thoughts. That's normal at the beginning. If you find yourself getting anxious, ask yourself these questions:

Am I breathing? If you can slow your breath, your body will automatically relax.

Am I relaxed? Move your body to a more comfortable position if not.

Am I open? You may be taking cues from your own positioning. Opening up may change how others view you as part of the group.

Challenging Yourself

Set goals for yourself. It's not enough to think "I'm gonna go out there and not be shy!" That isn't really a tangible goal -- that's similar to saying, "I want to be awesome." How do you do that? You need action-oriented goals, like talking to a stranger or initiating a conversation with a cute boy or girl you know. (We'll cover these actions in the next section).

Focus on small, daily accomplishments, then gradually become more daring. Even asking a stranger the time can be a daunting task. Don't write off these small chances as no big deal -- they're huge! You can work up to talking in front of huge crowds in a bit. Slow down!

Find what's comfortable for you. Straight up, moshing at a rave or drinking all night long at a club may not be for you -- that has nothing to do with shyness. If you'd rather be trimming your grandmother's toenails, listen to that. Don't try to conquer your shyness in environments you straight up can't stand. It won't stick.

You don't have to be doing what everybody else is doing. And if you do, you're not going to stick with it and you're not going to find people who you like and are similar to you. Why waste your time?! If the bar scene isn't for you, that's totally fine. Practice your social skills in coffee houses, at small gatherings, or at work. They're more applicable to your life.

Practice placing yourself in not-so-comfortable situations. Alright, so we don't want you in places where you are hiding in the corner pinching yourself to numb the social pain, but you do need to put yourself in environments where you're just a step or two out of your element. How else will you grow?

Start at the top of your list, remember? It could be making small talk with the CVS girl, stopping a person at the bus stop for the time, or chit-chatting it up with the guy who has the cubicle next to yours. Most people are crap at initiating (have you figured out why that is yet? They're just like you), but the opportunities for conversation are there.

Introduce yourself to one new person each day. It is often easier to talk with strangers, at least briefly. After all, you may never see them again, so who cares what they think about you? That guy down the street, walking to the bus. Try to make eye contact with him and smile. It's literally 3 seconds of your time!

The more you do this, the more you find that people are receptive and friendly. Once in a while, you'll get the occasional freak who's paranoid and wonders why you're smiling at him -- consider him just fun to mess with. What's more, smiling makes people wonder why you're smiling -- now you're getting in their heads instead of the other way around!

Put yourself out there. Talk to somebody you would not normally think about having a conversation with. Try to find people who share one or more of your interests and make plans to talk to them. At some point or another, you'll find yourself in front of a group. Chime in with even the most basic of statements (or in support of someone else's). Get involved. It's the only way to grow.

This will get easier with time. Remember how driving or riding a bike was hard at first? It's the same with social interactions; you just haven't had a lot of practice. After a while, you'll be all "been there, done that." Nothing will phase you.

Record your successes and keep going. In that notebook you have your social triggers listed, write down your successes. Seeing the progress you've made is a great motivation to keep going. In a few weeks, you'll be amazed at the control you're taking over this, convincing you all the more that this thing is doable. Awesome.

There is no timeline for this. For some people, it won't happen until a lightbulb clicks on and all of a sudden they get it. For others, it's a slow path that takes 6 months. However long it takes is however long it takes. Trust in yourself. You'll get there.

CHAPTER SEVEN
HOW TO STOP PANIC ATTACKS

A panic attack is a sudden and scary experience that can make you feel like you have a heart attack, that you are dying or that you are losing control. Many adults experience only 1 or 2 panic attacks in their life, but others have recurring attacks, which can be an indicator of an underlying problem called panic disorder. A panic attack is an abrupt onset of intense fear for no apparent reason, accompanied by very real physical changes, such as a fast heartbeat, very strong beats, sweat, and agitated breathing. You can follow some steps to stop a panic attack and to prevent other attacks from coming in the future.

Receive relief immediately

Recognize physical symptoms. During a panic attack, your body goes into a fight or flight reaction, as if you were in a really scary or dangerous situation, but in reality, no situation like that is happening. The symptoms that are usually experienced during a panic attack are as follows:

- Chest pain or discomfort

- Dizziness
- Afraid of dying
- Fear of losing control or experiencing an impending doom
- Choking sensation
- Feeling of indifference
- Feeling of unreality
- Nausea or upset stomach
- Numbness or tingling in the hands, feet or face
- Palpitations, fast heartbeat, strong beats
- Sweat, chills or hot flashes
- Tremors

Control you're breathing. Most panic attacks causes agitated and shallow breathing that fuels the attack, causing symptoms to last. By controlling your breathing, you can make your heart rate normal again, lower your blood pressure, sweat less and re-establish a feeling of being in control.

- One way to slow your breathing is to take a deep breath and hold your breath as much as you can. This balances the levels of oxygen and carbon dioxide and reduces the feeling that you cannot breathe.
- After holding your breath, start breathing deeply. Inhale slowly and deeply, and then exhale even more slowly.
- To practice diaphragmatic breathing, sit in a chair with one hand on your chest and the other a little

under your ribcage. Sit comfortably with your knees bent, and your shoulders and neck relaxed.

- Then, inhale slowly through your nose and let your stomach expand, keeping the upper part of your chest as still as possible. Exhale slowly, clenching your stomach muscles and keeping your upper chest still. The hand on your stomach should move as you inhale and exhale, while the hand on the upper part of your chest remains as still as possible.

- Another method is 5-2-5. Inhale with your diaphragm for 5 seconds. Hold your breath for 2 seconds. Then exhale for another 5 seconds. Repeat this process 5 times.

- It is no longer recommended to breathe in a paper bag. It may not be as favorable as previously believed, and could even be harmful.

Take prescription medication. One of the most effective ways to stop a panic attack is by taking oral agents classified as anti-anxiety medications.

- The medications that are normally used to treat panic attacks and that are classified as benzodiazepines are alprazolam, lorazepam, and diazepam. These agents have a relatively rapid onset and can help relieve symptoms between 10 and 30 minutes.

- Other prescription agents that are classified in the benzodiazepine group begin to function a little more slowly but remain in your blood flow longer. Some examples of these agents are clonazepam, chlordiazepoxide, and oxazepam.

- These agents are usually prescribed in smaller doses to be taken frequently until panic attacks become more controllable when using other types of medications, such as serotonin reuptake inhibitors or participation in cognitive behavioral therapy.

Continue with your activity. Continue with the activity you are doing and with your daily life as much as you can to prevent panic from consuming you.

- Keep talking, moving and concentrating on your thoughts. In doing so, you send messages to your brain and your panic, telling them that there is no danger, alarm or reason to put you in a state of struggle or flight.

Do not run away. If you have a panic attack in a specific place (maybe in a supermarket), then you might want to run away and leave the supermarket as quickly as possible.

By staying in that place and controlling your symptoms, you are taking steps to train your mind in order to recognize the absence of real danger in the supermarket.

If you run away, your brain begins to associate that place (and maybe all supermarkets) with danger and it can create feelings of panic every time you go to a supermarket.

Focus on other things. With the help of a therapist, you can learn ways to concentrate your thoughts on other things naturally and to control panic.

- For example, you can drink something warm or cold, walk a little, sing your favorite song, talk to a friend and watch TV.
- Other things you can do to focus on something other than panic are stretching exercises, putting together a puzzle, changing the temperature of the environment, lowering the window if you are in a car, going out for fresh air or reading something that interests you.

You must know how to distinguish between a stressful experience and a panic attack. Although both experiences are similar in the fact that physical reactions appear (such as high blood pressure, sweat, and an accelerated heart rate), they are very different.

- All people go through stressful moments at some point in their lives. The natural instinct of the fight or flight of the body could be activated in a stressful situation or that causes you anxiety, as well as in a panic attack, but there is always a trigger, event or experience that is directly related to the reaction.

- Panic attacks are not related to any event, they are unpredictable and the severity of an attack can be enormous and frightening.

Put into practice relaxation techniques. Follow steps to calm yourself down using established relaxation methods to control the situation that causes you too much stress or anxiety.

- If you suffer from panic attacks or a panic disorder, going to a cognitive behavioral therapist will help you learn relaxation techniques to control panic when it appears.

Use your senses to tackle the attack. Whether you experience a panic attack, anxiety or find yourself in a stressful situation, by concentrating on your senses, even if only for a moment, you can slow down the unwanted physical symptoms that appear.

- Use your sight to realize the pleasant things that surround you. If you are in a safe place, close your eyes and imagine your favorite flower, your favorite painting, your favorite beach or something that makes you feel more relaxed.
- Stop and listen to your surroundings. Find music from a distance, hear the birds, the wind or the rain, or even the noise of traffic or a nearby road. Find something new that you can hear, instead of listening to your palpitations and the sounds that are part of a stressful event.

- Keep using your senses to identify the smells around you. Maybe you are inside and someone is cooking or maybe you are outside and you can smell the rain.

- Focus on the sense of touch. You may not realize it, but you are always playing something. If you are sitting, focus on how you feel your chair or notice if the table on which your arms rest is cold or hot, or if you feel a breeze on your face.

- By taking those moments to review what your senses experience, you turn away your concentration of panic, anxiety or stress.

- This does not solve the cause of panic, anxiety or stress, but concentrating on your senses is useful for addressing the unwanted physical reaction your body may be experiencing.

Prevent future attacks

Talk to your doctor about your attacks. Your doctor can treat you with recommended medications or can refer you to a mental health professional to evaluate and prescribe medications. Both doctors will recommend a cognitive-behavioral therapist.

- Usually, many panic attacks are related to other underlying disorders, including some mental health problems and some medical problems. Talk to your doctor to rule out an underlying health problem.

Seek medical help as soon as possible. Some studies have shown that people who are treated with regard to panic attacks and disorders on time, get better results and fewer complications.

Take medications as prescribed. The agents that are normally used are benzodiazepines, both fast-acting and intermediate-acting.

- Benzodiazepines are considered addictive, so be sure to take them as prescribed by your doctor. Taking more than recommended is dangerous and can cause serious and potentially fatal effects if you take them too much.

Take quick-acting agents only when necessary. Quick-acting agents help you control your symptoms when you feel you are going to have a panic attack. They are usually prescribed for you to have on hand in case you need them or when you start having a panic attack.

- Take these agents only when necessary to avoid becoming tolerant of the prescribed dose.
- Some examples of the medications that are prescribed for you to take when you start having a panic attack, as needed, are lorazepam, alprazolam, and diazepam.

Take agents of a longer action on a regular basis or as recommended by the doctor. Intermediate action agents take a little longer to start acting but have more lasting effects.

- Usually, these medications are prescribed for you to take in your daily life, in order to help you avoid panic attacks until you can follow the next steps, such as cognitive-behavioral therapy.
- Some examples of intermediate-acting agents are clonazepam, oxazepam, and chlordiazepoxide.

Take an SSRI. Selective serotonin reuptake inhibitors, usually known as SSRIs, are effective in treating panic attacks and disorders.

- The SSRIs that are approved by the FDA for use in the treatment of panic symptoms are fluoxetine, fluvoxamine, citalopram, escitalopram, paroxetine, and sertraline. Duloxetine is an agent closely related to SSRIs and its use is also approved for the treatment of panic symptoms.

Go to a cognitive-behavioral therapist. This form of therapy is essential to train your mind and body to overcome panic attacks and to help you reach a point where they no longer appear.

- You should know what to expect from cognitive behavioral therapy. Therapists trained for this type of psychotherapy use 5 fundamentals when working with people suffering from panic attacks. Those 5 basics are:
- Learning about the disease helps you better understand what causes the terrifying symptoms you experience when you have a panic attack.

- Controlling and recording the dates and times of events, such as keeping a diary, helps you and the therapist to identify the causes of panic attacks.
- Breathing and relaxation techniques are part of the tools used to decrease the severity of symptoms.
- Reflection is used to change the perception of an attack so that it goes from being a catastrophic sensation to a realistic sensation.
- Exposing yourself in a safe and controlled manner to places and events that give rise to your attacks trains your mind and body to react in a different way.

Consider undergoing an evaluation for panic disorder. Panic disorder is diagnosed when four or more of the symptoms mentioned above occur.

- Early treatment for panic disorder improves overall outcomes and reduces possible complications related to constant attacks.

CHAPTER EIGHT

HOW TO TO INCREASE YOUR SELF-CONFIDENCE

Do you want to have more self-confidence? It is possible to increase self-confidence. Most experts agree that self-confidence is a combination of self-esteem and self-efficacy. Start by believing in yourself, your skills and your goals. This measure will help you deal with problems and stress factors, and simultaneously strengthen your self-confidence. Have a positive attitude, set quantifiable goals and keep the company of other people who have self-confidence and who are in solidarity. Then, you will be on track to develop it.

Set goals

Make a list of your strengths. This is a simple task that will help you acquire a positive mindset, which is essential to maintain self-confidence. Yes, you have areas that you need to improve, but everyone has them; However, often, lack of confidence comes from lack of self-esteem. Making a list of the positive aspects of your life can help you overcome the minor negative aspects. The following are some things you can include:

- Talents or abilities. It should not be competitive. It just means that you see yourself as a talented or skilled person in some areas, such as athletics, art, business or creativity.
- Personality traits. Take note of anything in your personality that you are proud of. For example, you may see yourself as someone who works hard, who cares or is imaginative.
- Achievements. These are things you have achieved that you are proud of. You may have participated in a concert, spoken in public, prepared a birthday cake or run in a race.

Understand your lack of self-confidence. Often, lack of self-confidence develops when you feel that the people in your life do not listen to you or do not support you. Often, this begins in early childhood and derives from family interactions. Maybe your parents were very critical, hard or punitive. This can impede the development of self-confidence and create anxious, indecisive and fearful adults who lack a sense of self. On the other hand, parents who overprotect their children also hurt them by not allowing them to try, fail, try again and finally succeed. The adult version is afraid to try anything new for fear of failure.

- For example, if your parents always criticized your efforts at school, it is likely that you have grown up believing that you are not intelligent or that you cannot succeed in life. You may think that others do not consider you an intelligent person or capable of working hard.

- If your parents never let you go anywhere alone when you were a child (for fear of being lost or kidnapped), you may have trouble as an adult to go to places you don't know. Actually, failure and the feeling of being lost is what makes a person learn.

Write what kind of self-confidence you want to have. Do you want to develop self-confidence to talk with people or in public? Write the areas in which you want to develop it. This can make your plan to have it clearer.

- For example, you probably want to talk to the class during a group project. You can also write that you would like to have more self-confidence when playing a group sport or doing some activity.

Create a simple action plan. Once you know in which area you want to develop self-confidence, specifically determine how you will do it. Maybe you should write the steps in the action plan. Start small and gradually ascend to more challenging situations or interactions.

- For example, write that you want to start a conversation with at least one person today. Ask a question in a class or in a group setting. Then practice talking with more people or asking more questions. Practicing is a vital part of developing self-confidence.

- You can plan to do interviews for three new jobs next year or apply for two new schools. In addition, your action plan may be smaller. Maybe your goal is to go out with friends once a week or take a class in which you are interested.

Set small and quantifiable goals. Make sure your goals are divided into detailed steps. In this way, you can track your progress. You will also feel that you have more self-confidence with these achievements. Make sure the goals are manageable and attainable.

- For example, a quantifiable goal with several steps can be something like the following: "Steps: train 6 months, run half marathon and train another 3 months. Goal: run a full marathon."
- Be sure to write and schedule the goals. This measure will increase the chances of achieving them. If you have problems, check the goal or think about what you have learned before moving on.

Develop self-confidence

Get the information you need. Depending on the area in which you would like to develop self-confidence, look for resources you may need. Find out if you will need formal training or education to achieve your goals. After all, it is difficult to have the self-confidence to fly a plane if you have not taken a lesson or if you have not sat in the pilot's seat. If you take a formal course, this can provide many opportunities to practice, which is another good way to develop self-confidence.

- Consider looking for a mentor, taking a class or reading about a topic you need to learn from. This measure will give you the tools you need to succeed.

Maintain a positive and optimistic attitude. Developing self-confidence requires that you stay focused and have a positive attitude. If people constantly criticize you or if your efforts go unnoticed, you will easily get discouraged. Take any negative questions you may have and turn it into positive statements or challenges. Create rituals for yourself in order to develop an internal dialogue or positive affirmations.

- For example, every morning when brushing your teeth, look at yourself in the mirror, smile and say something like "I will do my best today. I deserve to have self-confidence. "
- Do things you really enjoy. Listen to music, visit an art gallery, play basketball with some friends. Find out what you like to do and make sure you do it frequently. This measure will prevent negative doubts from returning.

Create a support network. A negative environment kills self-confidence. Find the company of people who support your efforts. In this way, you can freely practice self-confidence skills without the people around you judging you. Let your support network know that you are trying to develop self-confidence.

- If you have problems, do not hesitate to ask for help or support from a friend or family member.

Remind yourself of your strengths. Knowing that you have positive traits and qualities is a good thing, but without emphasizing and not focusing on these every day, you will soon return to the habit of insecurity and self-criticism. Keep the list of strengths in an easily accessible place so you can check it frequently. [16] Recite a mantra or statement that reminds you of your positive traits and abilities.

- For example, every time you use the bathroom, look in the mirror and say something nice about yourself. This will keep strengths in the mind firmly and increase self-confidence. Before you know it, you will feel comfortable with yourself and you will not be afraid of the opinions of others, which is one of the main qualities of a person who really has self-confidence.

Take educated risks. If you don't have a lot of self-confidence, you probably don't take many risks. On the other hand, people who have a lot of self-confidence can take reckless risks. Find a balance and take risks based on your skills and the reality of the situation. Taking educated risks can give your self-confidence a well-deserved boost.

- Taking risks means different things to each person. Maybe you want to go to a social activity that you would otherwise be afraid to go or maybe you want to risk confronting a friend who constantly bothers you. Try to give yourself the opportunity to enjoy new social situations or to leave the harmful ones.

Maintain self-confidence in difficult situations

Handle rejection. Understand that rejection is part of life. Although it hurts, you can stand up and go on with your life. Learn to handle it with elegance. For example, respond kindly and accept that you have been rejected. Respect the other person's decision and you will look like someone who has self-confidence and good self-esteem.

- Do not give up. Just because you missed a relationship, a job offer or a promotion, you shouldn't stop trying. Learn from rejection and move on.

Handles bullying (or abuse). Defend yourself. Bullies (or abusers) will continue to bother you if you leave them. Instead, face them and trust your support system. [19] Handles bullying showing self-confidence and courage. Tell the bully clearly to stop.

- Do not accept bullying as part of your life. Bullying is a bad thing and you have the right to live a life free of it, even if you have to talk to the head of the boss or the school principal to change the situation.

Manage a job interview . Self-confidence is essential when it comes to job interviews. Employers are constantly looking for someone who seems to have self-confidence and be competent. While it is easy to feel overwhelmed and nervous in an important event, one of the best things you can do is pretend that you have self-confidence. As you feel more comfortable, you will feel increasingly relaxed and with an attitude of true self-confidence.

- Listen and reaffirm during the interview. You don't feel simply answering questions. Instead, try to connect with the interviewer and let him know your goals. This measure will make it appear that you have self-confidence and that you pay attention.

Manage public speech. Entire books have been written on the subject of preparing and conducting an effective discourse, but as with most human interaction, one of the key elements of public speaking success is self-confidence. Consider trying the following strategies to develop self-confidence:

- Be funny. Humor can relax both you and the audience, and relieve any tension. The audience can also show more interest and have more confidence in you.

- Express self-confidence. Even if you feel you don't have self-confidence, use gestures and tones that denote it. Speak loudly and clearly, and use your arms to refer to the main points. Avoid slouching, babble or cross your arms.

- Make eye contact. This will make the audience pay attention and look like you have self-confidence. Try to find some people who look like they have a real interest in the speech and focus on them, not on those who seem uninterested.

Take care of yourself

Take into account the importance of self-care. Often, when a person lacks self-confidence, the attitude towards self-preservation is reduced to "Who really cares?" It should matter to you. Neglecting things like hygiene, health and time management is a sure way to make your lack of self-confidence worsen, as your ideal self gets more and more away from your reality.

- If you take better care of yourself, you will break the cycle and have a significant increase in self-confidence.

Practice good hygiene. Set aside a block of time each morning to comply with daily hygiene. Take a shower, wash your face, change your clothes and do whatever it takes to prepare for the day. When you are ready to go out the front door, you should feel that you have more self-confidence than usual.

- Keep up the routine every day to maintain that self-confidence.

Take care of your health. Simply put, eat a healthy diet that includes whole grains, fruits, vegetables, dairy products, and lean proteins. Limit alcohol and fatty foods, and do not overeat. Be sure to exercise regularly throughout the week.

- Stop smoking, especially if you resort to habit as an aid in social situations. Build trust by leaving it.

Manage the sleep schedule. It can be difficult to maintain a regular sleep schedule, especially during high school and college years. However, do your best to go to bed at the same time each night and get up at the same time each morning. Try to be awake at least one hour before you have to leave your home for work or for school.

You plan your day life around the time you spend sleeping, so the first step in organizing your day is to make sure you can get up at the same time each morning to continue with the schedule.

CHAPTER NINE

EMOTION ANXIETY

First of all, we must be clear that anxiety is a basic emotion. But what does this mean? That exists, in all people. It is not primary, like all we have seen before. It is important to keep in mind, in this emotion, that it recruits its resources from other emotional processes, for example, from fear it takes all its emotional elements, from stress its elicitation system ... And in this way, it takes resources from other psychological processes handling them at will.

WHAT DIFFERENTIATES ANXIETY FROM OTHER EMOTIONS?

Well, as we will see in the following section, anxiety occurs in threatening or dangerous situations. Do you remember what other emotions these triggers share? , indeed ..., it is with fear, so what makes this emotion different from the other? This happens because anxiety is generated before the threat becomes real. That is, only with the possibility of the existence of a possible threat, we feel anxious and fearful. Therefore, anxiety has an anticipatory character whose function is to avoid the appearance of these aversive stimuli. That is, if anxiety is adaptive and effective, fear has no place since the threat is eliminated.

As we have said before the possibility of threatening or harmful situations. These situations have been classified into four large blocks:

- Fear of interpersonal situations or events, including fear of criticism, rejection, social contact, etc ...
- Fears of rejection.
- Fear of animals.
- Fear of issues related to death, illness, injury, blood, and surgery.

Cognitive Processing of Anxiety

Due to the peculiarities of this emotion, it is important to note that anxiety produces effects of attentional, cognitive, memory bias. This means focusing our attention on those data that correspond to our anxious state. To make it easier to understand this point, we will give an example: imagine, that you have a special phobia of spiders and this degenerates into anxiety so that the simple fact of being in a situation in which increases the probability of crossing with a Spider will remind you of the movie you saw last week where killer spiders appeared. His anxious state produces a memory bias focusing attention on the object and bidder.

It has also been proven that anxiety produces biases in the interpretation of information. That is, before ambiguous stimuli, we tend to discard the neutral meaning and overestimate that of danger.

These biases in information processing result in the prioritization of issues. Something that is essential to escape from possible threatening situations or danger.

Physical effects

The physical effects that can be observed when we are under an anxious state can be classified in this way as presented below:

- Increased muscle tone
- Increased heart rate and blood pressure.
- Peripheral temperature drops.
- Increase in frequency and respiratory amplitude.
- Increased skin constancy.
- Increased adrenaline in the blood.

Subjective effects

The repertoire of emotional experiences associated with anxiety is very wide and varied depending on the individual differences of each person. However, anxiety is the subjective experience par excellence of anxiety. Along with it, other sensations appear such as worry, apprehension, discomfort, threat, difficulty concentrating, negative thoughts, inferiority complexes, and we can even experience on some occasions a state of panic.

Together with these subjective experiences, others of a physical nature produced by the first ones appear, including hot flashes, tremors, tension, choking sensations, sweats, etc.

Body expression

Being an emotion that combines resources and characteristics of other emotions, you can not distinguish typical facial patterns or distinctive body expressions. This is largely due to cultural differences. We must not forget that the expression of emotions is regulated by social learning.

However, if you can affirm some generalities. Among them are:

- Hyperactivity
- The clumsy movements.
- Disorganized behaviors

In addition to nonverbal communication, avoidance behaviors stand out. Some of them are:

Behaviors that manifest motor restlessness, such as carrying out activities without a purpose.

An excessive performance of behaviors such as smoking or drinking.

Behaviors that indicate discomfort, such as avoidance of gaze

Coping with anxiety

There are four coping styles whose central pillars are vigilance and cognitive avoidance.

The coping style characterized by low vigilance and high cognitive avoidance is characterized by its high tolerance for uncertainty and suffering large physiological changes as a result of this anxiety. The people who present this coping style are the repressive people, their behavior is the tendency to inhibit the processing of the threatening information since it ignores the indications of it on their own initiative.

The coping style defined by high vigilance and low cognitive avoidance is characterized by its low tolerance for uncertainty. The people who present this coping style are those known as sensitized, who tend to focus all their attention on the situations that cause their anxiety.

The coping style that presents low levels in both parameters. Both surveillance and cognitive avoidance are defined by their high tolerance both uncertainty, physiological activation. These people, called defensive or low in anxiety, use the coping resources that provide them with stress, allowing them to carry out a wide range of strategies. It must be said, that much lower levels of these parameters produce a remarkable insensitivity in the person to threatening situations which clearly goes against the adaptive nature of anxiety.

And finally, the coping style that is characterized by a high level of both vigilance and cognitive avoidance that is characterized by a low tolerance for both uncertainty and physiological activation, makes people known as highly anxious to experience continuous changes in activity This coping style is the least effective.

It should be noted that these are extreme trends in action, but coping styles are continuous, that is, anyone can be at any point at any time.

Pathological anxiety

Anxiety is associated with numerous psychological and psychiatric disorders, putting in most cases incapacitation to enjoy and be able to lead a full and healthy life.

These disorders include:

Generalized anxiety disorder, generates a state of excessive worry that can not be controlled in a wide variety of situations such as work performance.

Panic disorder, unforeseeable episodes associated with palpitations, chest pain, dizziness, shortness of breath occur. With the passage of time, those affected present anticipated anxiety and avoid any contact with the object or the situation that causes them anxiety.

Agoraphobia is an irrational fear of being in open places. People affected by these types of disorders are unable to develop a normal life and to carry out activities such as day-to-day shopping or going to university or any activity outside their space.

Social phobia, fear of social contact for fear of the evaluation of other people.

Phobic disorders, unlike other disorders associated with anxiety, these types of pathologies have very specific triggers. However, their avoidance alters the social normality of the person suffering from it.

Obsessive-compulsive disorder anxiety is the result of obsessions that are relieved only by the execution of compulsive behaviors. The best-known example is that of people who have a special dread to be the target of germs and who wash their hands compulsively, some acquired manias are difficult to eliminate without help.

It is not that anxiety is maladaptive, anxiety in certain situations that can be dangerous is very useful and effective. However, the problem occurs when this reaction occurs to inappropriate stimuli.

Discover how the body helps you discover your emotions

How do emotions influence your body?

The body and emotions go hand in hand when one speaks the other reacts. There are numerous scientific investigations that support the influence of emotions on pain and the physical body and how they are constantly related. In fact, it has been shown that similar areas of the brain are activated when we experience physical pain and emotional pain.

For example, if you do not manage anger or the stress of your work, this can sometimes lead to contracture or tension in the jaw. They are unexpressed emotions, which remain embedded in your body, waiting for you to let them out. As they cannot manifest themselves, they will try to express themselves in some way, and end up doing so in the form of physical tensions or discomforts.

In fact, the body is a map that helps us know what we are feeling. Surely it has ever happened to you, that you have noticed a lump in your throat when there was something you were not saying to your partner. Or for example, you have noticed a stomachache, feeling afraid of facing an exam. These are signals that the body gives you to express your emotions.

Emotions scream when we don't listen to them and transform into pain and physical suffering. What message does our body have to convey to us? Some symptoms such as headache, shortness of breath, feeling overwhelmed, stomach knot ...

Although we try to ignore them, the physical sensations are still there, the less we pay attention to them, the worse it is because they express themselves with greater intensity.

Many times we try to cover these pains or sensations with pills, which momentarily relieve our pain. However, they don't solve it; We only put a band-aid on a wound that is not healed, because emotions still cannot express themselves properly. Wouldn't it be better if we could attend to the emotional message that these bodily sensations want to convey to us?

Imagine a boy who works 15 hours a day, and has so much stress that he gets up with contractures in his neck every day. Even so, he takes a muscle relaxant and keeps working. Surely, the message your body is transmitting is that you need to stop, slow down and take breaks.

Pay attention to your physical pain to see what your body needs, if you learn to manage your emotions, you will be much better also physically.

Each emotion is linked to physical sensations in the body

I will deepen the physical sensations that the four basic emotions usually generate. In addition, I will also explain how to manage emotions so that they do not end in intense physical pain.

1. Fear

It is an emotion that warns us of possible dangers and helps us anticipate and protect ourselves from a possible threat. On a physical level, fear is expressed with stomach pain, body tension, the heart is racing, sweating, chest pressure, diarrhea, appetite changes, and insomnia among others.

All these symptoms are not exclusive to fear, but they can be present in this emotion that sometimes is so limiting.

If you feel any of these bodily sensations, you can check whether the emotion you are feeling is fear or another. In order to manage fear, it is best that instead of avoiding it, try to face it as it comes. For example, if you have to make a presentation in public, you can practice breathing and relaxation techniques that help you manage your fear.

2. Angry

Anger is the emotion that helps us to take action and defend our rights when we feel that an injustice has been committed. Among the most common physical symptoms are body tension, acceleration of the breathing , jaw tension, body temperature rise, headaches, etc.

These physical sensations can indicate to us that we are frustrated and it is necessary that we learn to manage this emotion in an assertive way since many times it can be repressed. For example, if your partner has bothered you, I have told you that you leave your clothes without picking up instead of shouting at it, or shut up and say nothing, you could, after being calmer, explain how you feel.

3. Joy

This emotion helps us establish links to socialize and share our happiness with others. Joy has physical symptoms that are easily recognizable: facial smile, chest expansion, laughter, body opening, etc. There are people who have difficulty feeling this pleasant emotion and do not know how to identify it.

4. Sadness

It is an emotion that helps us face losses and duels. It picks us up and makes us reflect on the past, and how things went. On a physical level, it is expressed with tears, sobs, chest pressure, shortness of breath, poor appetite, etc. Sensations that we all may have experienced at some point.

If sadness is not expressed it can become an unbearable weight to carry in our body. For example, if you have not cried the death of a loved one, or been able to share your pain with anyone, sadness may appear in the form of backaches or in some other part of your body.

Your body is wise and knows what you need

If we manage our emotions in a healthy way, we can listen and understand the message that our body sends us. We will identify the emotions associated with physical symptoms, and we will learn to manage these emotions so that they do not become unbearable physical pain.

Think that your body helps you to know yourself better if you learn to interpret your hidden emotional messages and give it what it needs (rest, attention, exercise, etc.).

You only need to open your gaze to your physical part so that this is an important part of your life. Your body is wise and knows what you need. If you take care of your body you also take care of your emotions. Remember that with your body you will live a lifetime, therefore, it is worth paying more attention and care. Thus, you will not only improve your emotional intelligence. but also your body consciousness.

CHAPTER TEN

HOW TO CONTROL EMOTIONS

Do you decide how to control emotions?

There are many theories about it. Some psychologists believe that we have total control over our emotions and others believe that there is no possibility of controlling them.

However, there is research that concludes that the way you interpret your emotions can change the way you live them. The way you react to a specific emotion will determine how it acts on you.

The speaker who suffers from the idea of public speaking does so because he interprets his nerves as something negative, as a signal that his body is sent to run away from there.

On the other hand, someone who interprets those same nerves as excitement and desire to do well will probably be more successful in his lecture.

The moral is that your body gives you the energy to do something, but how to use that energy is decided by you. There are people who pay money and queue hours to get on a roller coaster, while others would not ride even in dreams. Both feel the same nerves, but interpret them differently: fun in the face of terror.

What happens when your emotions get out of control

You can't help feeling emotions. Emotions are there because they have an evolutionary function, a biological sense of survival. If our ancestors had not felt fear in front of a herd of tigers, probably the human being would not have arrived until today.

The tonsil is the part of your brain that triggers emotions as if it were an automatic response in the form of aggression or flight in the face of a threat. That is why it is so difficult to control the origin of your emotions through willpower: it would mean canceling this answer for which you are genetically programmed.

This type of emotional response is therefore necessary. However, in some people, it is not properly regulated and it may happen that:

Shoot in situations where there is no real threat (causing anxiety)

Be unable to deactivate over time (as in depression). For some reason, the brain enters survival mode and remains anchored there.

When you are in the fight-flight phase and the amygdala has taken command of your actions, it is usually too late. That is why you must learn to act before. You have to get used to detecting those signals that tell you that you are on your way to not being able to master your emotions.

This is the only way you will be able to stop the process (or delay it) before it is too late. Once emotions dominate you, you are little more than a cornered beast.

The truth about negative emotions

The most recent theory is that there are 4 types of basic emotions that have evolved into the rest of more complex feelings. These emotions are anger , fear , joy, and sadness .

There are some situations that you can never get used to. If everything goes wrong, you can hardly leave behind the feeling of fear or anxiety. However, positive emotions usually disappear over time. No matter how much money you touch in the lottery or how in love you are: positive emotions such as pleasure always end up diminishing.

In fact, in one study it was determined that the emotion that lasts the longest is sadness . Specifically, it lasts up to 4 times longer than joy.

Based on this panorama it seems really necessary to be able to manage the intensity of your emotions so as not to suffer so much. Below you will find a list of the techniques that have not demonstrated any efficacy and those that have.

What does not work to control your emotions

These techniques have been popularized through word of mouth and by authors who have not bothered to verify their real scientific basis. The usefulness of each of them to manage your emotions is, at least, doubtful.

1. Try not to think about what worries you

In the same way that trying not to think of a white polar bear will cause you to end up thinking about it because of a rebound effect, in studies like this, it has been shown that it is very difficult to remove emotions from our head.

In the case of depressed people, who are constantly assaulted by negative thoughts, it has been proven that it is totally counterproductive to try to suppress those ideas because they end up returning even more strongly.

2. Relax and take a deep breath ...

It is usual to recommend us to relax and take a deep breath when we are angry or very anxious. It comes from an almost ancestral tradition, such as breathing inside a plastic bag in a panic attack.

But there is an inconvenience. Taking a deep breath and trying to modulate the diaphragm does not usually work because the physiological component of emotions is usually unimportant.

Think about it. In most of the occasions when you have become very angry, for example, you were calm before you became irascible. You probably had a good day until someone has crushed you, am I wrong?

If a previous state of relaxation has not prevented you from getting angry, why do people think they can get it once you're angry?

Have you ever recommended someone to relax when he was angry? You will have noticed that it does not usually work too well. It is as if instead of listening to those who believe they have suffered an injustice, you should be quiet and take a tranquilizer.
By this, I do not mean that using relaxation techniques is usually bad. In fact, meditating is quite useful (see below). But trying to relax once your emotions have invaded you is to treat the symptom and not the cause.

3. Release tension by other means

There was a time when activities to release emotions became fashionable. Workshops where people gathered to cry or events where aggressive managers began to break dishes.

Well, it turns out that the most recent psychological studies suggest that this type of catharsis does not work. It can even be negative: succumbing to the temptation to destroy everything can increase your aggressiveness in the short term. The same goes for physical exercise: although it is good for your heart, it is not able to calm your emotions.

Emotions are not contained within our body and need to come out as if we were pressure cookers. What they need is to be understood to avoid being harmed.

4. Press to have positive thoughts

There is some controversy regarding the effect of optimistic thoughts to regulate emotions. While I would not say that they are able to make your move from a negative to a positive state, they can reduce the intensity of negative emotion.

Emotions are processed almost entirely at the unconscious level and then go to the conscious ground, where you perceive them. For this reason, when you are aware of them it is often too late.

However, looking for the positive part of each situation can prevent you from continuing to sabotage yourself. If instead of thinking "I will not be able to do this" you begin to believe "It is complicated, but I can handle it" you will prevent your negative emotions from getting worse.

What does work

True emotional intelligence requires that you identify and understand your own moods. It involves recognizing when and why you are angry, nervous or sad, and act on the causes and not just the symptoms.

However, on those occasions when you see that you are inevitably moving towards a negative emotional state, the following techniques can be effective in stopping or curbing that chain reaction.

Try to remember your virtues and successes

The reaffirmation of your strengths and strengths is one of the best strategies to manage your feelings. It consists of thinking about what caused that emotion but reducing its negative meaning.

Example: instead of getting angry because you are late for work you may think that, since you are always on time, it is not so serious.

People with greater emotional control use self-affirmation when the intensity of their emotions is still low and they have time to look for another point of view of the situation. Interestingly, it has been shown that this strategy works especially well in women.

The next time you feel you lose control over your emotions, remind yourself of those things you take pride in your life.

Distract your attention to a specific issue

People who best manage their emotions have also learned to use distraction to block their emotional states before it is too late. And it seems to be very effective when they anticipate that they will experience intense emotions and do not have enough time to use other strategies.

Think about your most immediate future

Very intense emotions can cause you to forget that there is a future and that your actions will have consequences. Although at that moment you are only able to live the present and your frustration, anger or nerves seem so important to you, will you still feel that in a week?

Thinking about the immediate future is very effective in maintaining self-control, as demonstrated in the popularized experiment through the book Emotional Intelligence. In it, children who resisted the temptation to eat a treat in exchange for receiving another one got better results in school tests and better jobs in the coming years.

Meditate regularly

Meditation has proven scientifically effective in preventing repetitive negative thoughts and not only while meditating, but also in the long term: it is able to decrease the level of activation of the tonsil permanently.

Meditation also has studied in reducing anxiety. In one of them, four 20-minute meditation classes were enough to reduce anxiety by 39%.

Trying to relax only when your emotions assail you is not very effective. However, meditating regularly and breathing correctly can reduce the intensity of negative emotions when they appear.

Give yourself permission to worry later

I have explained to you before that trying to suppress an emotion or thought causes it to come back stronger. However, postponing it for later may work!

In one study, participants with anxious thoughts were asked to postpone their concern for 30 minutes. Despite being an alternative way to avoid thinking about something, what has been shown is that after this period of pause the emotions return with much less intensity.

So, give yourself permission to worry after a timeout. You will worry less.

Think about the worst thing that can happen to you

Do you remember the movie Unforgiven (Unforgiven) by Clint Eastwood?

In it, the character of William Munny, despite being old and finished, is the best gunman in the west. And it is not because of its speed or its aim. As he says, it is because when the bullets start to fly, he controls his emotions and keeps calm.

But how to keep calm? The samurai and the Stoics kept calm even in the most dramatic situations, how did they get it?

Write a diary of your emotions

The expressive writing is to write about your thoughts and feelings deeper and proven to be effective both psychologically and physically (it is able to accelerate the healing of wounds!)

Keeping a kind of emotional diary about what you've felt in some situations will help you reduce the recurrence of negative thoughts.

Take a break (and a soda) to regain self-control

Your self-control is not infinite. In fact, several investigations indicate that as you expose yourself to situations and emotions, it is consumed.

Think of it as sprinting. After the race, you are exhausted and need time to recover before running again. In the same way, if you manage to master your emotions, avoid re-exposing yourself to a tense situation or you will be more likely to succumb.

The most surprising thing is that it has been shown that maintaining control consumes glucose, as if you were literally exercising. Therefore, to recover your self-control you have two strategies:

Drink a sugar-rich drink (no kidding).

Use positive reaffirmation to manage your emotions again (source).

The key is to identify when your levels of self-control are low and avoid more emotional situations while you recover.

When all else fails, look for a mirror

Sorry? Looking in a mirror? Yes, as surprising as this strategy may seem, it can be useful to placate you when you are furious.

Several studies have shown that when you see yourself reflected you are able to observe yourself from a more objective perspective and therefore separate for a few moments of your emotionality.

The more aware you are of what you are doing, the more ability to control your emotions. And watching you in a mirror will increase your levels of self-awareness and help you behave more socially.

The most important thing: find the reason for your emotions

In the long term, the key is not to fight your emotions but to recognize them and know why they happen to you. For example:

"Ok, I don't like feeling that way but right now I am very envious (you recognize the emotion) because Andres has been congratulated for his work and I don't (you recognize why) ."

CONCLUSION

While all the social situations we go through are never the same, we can choose how to respond to those situations. We can avoid social commitments due to feelings of inferiority or inadequacy, of worrying about what others think of us. Or we can look at social invitations as opportunities to develop our own interpersonal skills and with minimal effort, we can become more and more comfortable in each new meeting or event.